The Jesse Jackson Phenomeno

The Jesse Jackson Phenomenon

The Crisis of Purpose in Afro-American Politics

ADOLPH L. REED, JR.

Yale University Press
New Haven and London

Designed by Susan P. Fillion
and set in Times Roman text and Memphis
display type, and printed and bound in the
United States of America, by The Maple-Vail Book
Manufacturing Group.

Library of Congress Cataloging-in-Publication Data

Reed, Adolph L., 1947–
    The Jesse Jackson phenomenon.

    Includes index.
    1. Afro-Americans—Politics and government.
2. Jackson, Jesse, 1941–   . 3. Presidents—
United States—Election—1984. 4. United States—
Politics and government—1981–   . I. Title.
E185.615.R38   1986   973.927'0924   85-26499
ISBN 0-300-03543-8 (alk. paper)
ISBN 0-300-03552-7 (pbk. : alk. paper)

*The paper in this book meets the guidelines
for permanence and durability of the
Committee on Production Guidelines
for Book Longevity of the Council on
Library Resources.*

10 9 8 7 6 5 4 3 2 1

To the members of Locals 34 and 35 of the Federation of University Employees, who, while this book was being written, acted with great courage to advance a concrete vision of human dignity.

Contents

Preface

In January 1984 I decided to write an irate letter to the editor of the *Nation,* an unsolicited reply to a panegyric about Jesse Jackson's recently announced presidential candidacy. Then things began happening so quickly in the campaign that by the southern primaries the most reasonable course seemed to be to forgo the letter and wait until after the Democratic convention to do a more systematic assessment of Jackson's initiative. Toward the end of the summer I began writing what I thought was a conference paper on the Jackson campaign and its significance in the present state of Afro-American politics. After four months of often round-the-clock obsession the letter to the editor had transformed itself, almost behind my back, into this book.

As I began to write, it became ever clearer that Jackson's candidacy and the reactions it engendered—for example, from other black political elites, national news media, and the white

Left and liberal-Left—captured in a single moment several important conditions and tendencies driving Afro-American politics in the 1970s and 1980s. Thus, the Jackson phenomenon became simultaneously a topic for examination in its own right and a window onto the larger dynamics that have structured post–civil rights era black political activity in general. Most prominent among these are: (1) the development of competing criteria for legitimation of claims to black political leadership; (2) the sharpening of lines of socioeconomic stratification within the Afro-American population; and (3) the growth of centrifugal pressures within and external attacks on the national policy consensus represented in the Democratic coalition, which has been the main context for articulation of black political agendas for at least a generation. The central thesis of this book is that the 1984 Jesse Jackson phenomenon must be understood not only in relation to these dynamics; the Jackson phenomenon also is emblematic of the inadequacy of conventional patterns of discourse concerning black political activity, which originate in a pre–civil rights context of racial protest, for generating either critical interpretations or appropriate strategic responses in the present situation.

Several friends and colleagues have been valuable sources of information, criticism, and insight. They include: Elizabeth Alexander, Harold Barnette, Gerald Jaynes, Martin Kilson, Jim Lee, Willie Legette, Laughlin McDonald, Katherine McFate, my parents Adolph Reed, Sr., and Clarita M. Reed, Steven Rosenstone, Ian Shapiro, Preston Smith, Rogers Smith, Clarence Stone, Mary Stone, and especially Alex Willingham, whose encouragement and counsel concerning this project from its inception are only the most recent manifestations of a comradeship that stretches back to the Charlie Scott era at the University of North Carolina. All these people have contributed to this study's strengths; however, in the spirit of civic equality it is only proper that at least some of them share my responsibility for its limitations. A desire to keep open the option to impose on them in the future preserves the anonymity of the culpable.

I should also acknowledge the contributions of the participants in the Political Theory Seminar and the Afro-American Studies Faculty Colloquium at Yale, as well as of the graduate students in my Afro-American Social Thought seminar in the fall of 1984 and my Twentieth-Century American Political Thought seminar in the spring of 1985. I have presented parts of this manuscript in each of those settings, and the final product has been enriched by my various coseminarians' comments.

In addition, I am indebted to Kathleen Frankovic and Cary Funk of the CBS News Election and Survey Unit for their responsiveness in sharing unpublished poll data with me. Steve Suitts of the Southern Regional Council was patient and supportive both in providing current data on southern voting and in helping me to unravel the web of technicalities and conventions surrounding analysis of political participation in the region. Brian Sherman, then with the Voter Education Project, and Tom Cavanagh, then at the Joint Center for Political Studies, were equally patient with my more frequent intrusions into their normal activities. I wish to thank each of those individuals and organizations for their assistance. Of course, they are in no way implicated in any of the arguments that I put forth in this volume.

Marian Ash and her colleagues at Yale University Press—Ruth Kummer, Maura D. Shaw Tantillo, and Michael Joyce—have been most encouraging and congenial. Their enthusiasm for this project and despatch in handling it are deeply appreciated. Similarly, Tanya Coke, whose talents as a research assistant come to me through Yale's Afro-American Studies program, has been the answer to a novena. Without the acuity of judgment, self-direction, and thoroughness with which she prepared this volume's index, production timetables would have failed.

Moving closer to home, loved ones (who share initials, and little else, to be sure, with Teddy Roosevelt) were forced to endure the fallout from the obsessive "twenty-page-paper-that-wouldn't-end." One responded with encouragement, reassurance, and the equanimity that he wears as a family crest; the other shared her compassion, emotional support, occasional frustration, and untold hours of critical discussion of my arguments. To the two TRs: Let me herewith record my great appreciation for the sacrifices and adjustments (as if there were not already enough) that I thrust upon you because of this project over the fall term of 1984. I am glad we all survived it, and I hope this book is worthy of the burdens you shouldered for it.

Finally, I have reserved special thanks for Mrs. Jeanne J. Rose, who volunteered to prepare a manuscript that we thought would be about a third as long as it turned out to be. As she worked on the draft, it grew and grew. Nevertheless, she gave her time and consummate skills most generously. Moreover, Mrs. Rose was one of the first to suggest that the project should be recast as a book and was the first actually to read the draft. Through the arduous months of writing, her excitement about and critiques of my output, combined with my respect for her willingness to extend herself on my behalf, redoubled my perseverance. In more than one sense, therefore, she is intimately connected with this project's fruition.

1

The Context of Elite Competition

The central fact of the Jackson phenomenon has gone unnoticed: that it was a ritualistic event—a media-conveyed politics of symbolism, essentially tangential to the critical debate over reorganization of American capitalism's governing consensus.[1] The defense that Jackson brought hope to the dispossessed offers no consolation; rather, it repeats the unsophisticated conventional wisdom that black people require symbolic politics instead of routinized programmatic politics. In what follows I shall examine the various claims made by and for the campaign with a dual objective: (1) to determine the legitimacy of each claim on its face and (2) to demonstrate the more fundamental problems of which those claims are emblematic. The most important are the mercurial category of Afro-American "leadership" that organizes discussion of black politics, the nature of political discourse and the crisis of political agenda in the black com-

1

munity, and the patronizing orientations that define the place
of blacks in the purview of liberals and the Left.

Jackson and Black Leadership Legitimation

Jackson's claim to legitimacy as a contender for the Democratic nomination was from the first connected with his assertion of authenticity as a spokesman for black interests.
Predictably, this assertion met mixed reactions from the ranks
of nationally visible black elected officials. Many of the latter, most notably the mayors Coleman Young of Detroit and
Andrew Young of Atlanta, opposed Jackson's gambit, contending that he had usurped the role of elected officials in
brokering black political interests.[2] As the campaign snow-
balled—fueled by images of Jackson purportedly appealing
directly to the black "masses," via a church network, and
over the heads of entrenched political elites—most of these
critics were won over, subdued, or silenced. Yet, an anomaly
posed in the early opposition remained. Though his claims to
political leadership never had been subjected to the empirical
test of ratification by any electorate in any jurisdiction (for
that matter he had only recently registered to vote), Jesse
Jackson was on the way to becoming—at least for the moment—the central black personality in Democratic party politics.

The circumspection of black elected officials on one level
reflects an underlying dynamic in post–civil rights era black
politics. Since the mid-1960s a combination of demographic
shift and removal of restrictions to black voter participation
has resulted in the rise of a group of elected politicians whose
assumptions of spokesmanship status are based on officially
validated relations to specifically identifiable black constituencies. Even though the more aggressive claims of this
group—for example, Coleman Young's contention that, by
virtue of the scope of their officeholding, black big-city may-

ors should have priority as articulators of national black interests—tend to overstep their limited jurisdictional mandates, it is nonetheless the case that elected officials are the only claimants to black political leadership status who are held accountable for their actions by the presence of unambiguous mechanisms for popular ratification within the Afro-American community.

Several observers have examined the significance that this stratum's growth and consolidation has for the character of Afro-American politics. Ronald Walters[3] and Robert Smith[4] have argued in somewhat different ways that the rise of elected officialdom has regularized black political participation and provided a set of concrete, systemic avenues for expression and realization of black interests. Both authors see newly opened electoral channels as a natural and efficacious outgrowth of protest and other extrasystemic forms that characterized pre–Voting Rights Act black politics. The logical implication of their interpretations is that elected officials should be seen as the principal bearers of black political interests, although Smith and Walters became early supporters of and fervent activists in Jackson's campaign. Martin Kilson notes that the number of elected officials has reached a critical mass capable of sustaining formal political linkage institutions— Congressional Black Caucus, National Conference of Black Mayors, and so forth—that solidify blacks' structural integration into national and local public policy processes.[5] These new developments, all observers agree, have altered the strategic basis of black political activity by creating an elite division of labor in which political officials have primary responsibility for conversion of black concerns into legitimate public policy agenda items.

These interpretations proceed, certainly, from a functionalist view that defines the objectives of black extrasystemic politics exclusively in relation to the pressing of black interest claims. However, given the practical outcomes of civil rights and black power activism and the programmatic orientation of the general black protest lobby, that functionalism has a sound empirical basis.[6] In fact, the empirical soundness of the functionalist interpretation is the basis for a deeper cleavage underlying prominent politicians' initially lukewarm response to Jackson's proposed candidacy: a tension between the newer cohort of elected officials and the "traditional" protest elite.[7]

Black Leadership Diversification in the Post-Voting Rights Era

The functions of the protest elite—custodians of the organizational apparatus that brokered black political interests prior to the rise of elected officialdom—have become increasingly ambiguous in the face of consolidation of electorally defined linkage mechanisms. To the extent that the extraelectoral political style centered in the civil rights organizations has as its only public object pressing black claims within established policy processes, it is not clear where those organizations stand in relation to electoral elites. At stake is the relative status of the two groups as legitimate definers of black interests and, of course, as recipients of the benefits of that status. In this context the widely advertised August 1983 celebration commemorating the twentieth anniversary of the March on Washington can be read as an attempt by an element of the protest elite to assert itself by emphasizing its links to heroic activism in the civil rights movement. This reading might help to make sensible the reluctance, and outright refusal, of many within political elite circles to support that commemorative effort.[8]

This cleavage suggests one dimension of the Jackson phenomenon. By 1981 the uncertain relations between electoral and protest elements had become an object of explicit black elite concern, spurred in part by Reaganism's unsettling impact. A conscious effort began under the impetus of the Congressional Black Caucus (CBC), Andrew Young, and others to formalize a national leadership structure from the ranks of political elites and racial advocacy organizations within the rubric of a "black leadership family."[9] This effort emphasized the diversity of specialized roles filled by the various components of the post–civil rights era black political elite, and a generally expressed theme was the need to dispense with the notion that a central, individual spokesperson is either possible or historically appropriate. Ironically, Rev. Walter Fauntroy, the District of Columbia's nonvoting delegate to the House of Representatives and then Chair of the CBC, and Roger Wilkins were among the more forceful proponents of this latter view. Fauntroy announced, "We do not have a single black leader, nor do the times dictate that there be."[10] Wilkins concluded a survey of the challenges facing blacks in the current period with equal forthrightness: "What we don't need is a new, media-appointed leader."[11] Within less than three years both had proclaimed Jesse Jackson the embodiment of collective black aspirations!

Despite the ecumenical pronouncements of the conveners of the "black leadership family," however, this effort could not overcome the fundamental internal pressures within the leadership elite. The call for formalization of a national structure was connected with what Kilson describes as the processes of "modernization" at work in contemporary black politics.[12] In the context of a modernizing tendency, political roles are regularized and allocated on the basis of effective specialization and relation to particular constituencies. Thus, the "family" rhetoric coexisted with a recurrent call for mobilizing black professionals on a consultantship basis to deploy their "expertise" to meet the complex contemporary issues.[13] This focus implicitly demoted the traditional protest elite, whose claims to leadership status derived from essentially different and irreconcilable criteria. In a charge to develop a new, middle class-based "technical militance," Joseph Madison, an NAACP functionary, exemplified the contradiction in comments at the CBC conference that convoked the "leadership family." By condescendingly suggesting the obsolescence of the "technical militance" appropriate to the civil rights era, Madison indirectly called into question the propriety of leadership claims by the stratum associated with extraelectoral protest politics.[14]

At the level of empirical politics, the basis of the contradiction lies in the pluralist porkbarrel. The protest elite has not generated a political vision or an agenda extending beyond lobbying for race-identifiable increments within the broader social policy frameworks as they are presently defined. To that extent, the growth of black linkage mechanisms institutionalized around formal officeholding on the one side increases the number of black hands dipping into the same barrel. On the other, because of their greater ability both to deliver payoffs to constituents and to mobilize and sustain support at the grass roots and elsewhere, official elites are capable of more effective action at this level of politics. Inasmuch as the protest elite seeks to occupy the same brokerage niche that it filled in the pre–Voting Rights Act period, it becomes increasingly redundant and potentially superfluous.

A possible alternative is proposed by Ronald Walters, who—like Kilson—finds elective elites superior in advancing racially identified objectives through systemic political processes. Walters argues that the presently appropriate role for civil rights organizations entails creating extrainstitutional pressure that "softens" the system for the manipulation of official black elites.[15] Though reasonable on its face, this strategy is naive in that it does not account for a major obstacle that blocks its realization. This obstacle is two-dimensional and inherent in the protest elite's elemental core. On the ideological plane the protest leadership lost its critical edge with the success of 1960s activism in securing avenues for black middle-class integration into the pluralist distributive queue. That success neutralized the protest stance, because once the major concessions were received (passage of public accommodations and voting rights legislation, official legitimation of an affirmative action apparatus that protects middle-class mobility) there was a reduction of extrasystemic or oppositional issues as the focus of racial activism. The major remaining function, given the limited character of racial protest critique, was ongoing administrative negotiation of the forms and levels of black inclusion. Moreover, once public accommodations and voting rights victories were secured, the protest agenda lost its collectively racial aspect and became an increasingly exclusive engine for advancing middle-class interests.[16] This development is significant ideologically because as the scope of demands for black inclusion narrows to the manageable category of middle-class interest, protest advocacy becomes increasingly functional, eschewing antisystemic militancy.

The uncoupling of the black middle-class agenda undermines the possibility of the protest leadership's assumption of a key role on the practical political plane as well. Extrasystemic protest activity depends on mass mobilization, and a program that reduces only to increasing the leverage of black elites simply will not generate active, widespread popular black support—no matter how many variations of cynical ideologies of "role models" and "positive images" are deployed to create illusions of collective racial interest. Moreover, the protest elite itself has little real interest in mass politics; the major racial advocacy organizations operate ever more frequently as appendages of state and foundation apparatus, deriving large shares of their budgets from administering public programs as delegate agencies and occasionally as line items in public budgets. Moreover, this administrative function is legitimated ultimately by the civil rights elites' claims to an organic *political* relation to the black population. Although infusions of professionalistic ideologies into racial management functions may invest the protest element with more explicitly bureaucratic legitimations, it is most unlikely under present circumstances that the tension between official and protest elites can be resolved because they compete for places in the same niche.

Jackson's presidential candidacy connects with this tension in several interesting ways. The early negative response by elected officials to Jackson's campaign probably grew from a number of sources. Harold Washington, for example, had been trying to distance himself from Jackson since the Chicago mayoral primary a year earlier, and for reasons that mainly concerned Chicago politics.[17] The Youngs and others, as long-time Democrats, already were committed to Mondale through party linkages and felt Jackson's initiative to be disruptive. The primacy of black Democratic politicians' party loyalty is a natural consequence of the regularization of electoral participation and has been a clear limitation on insurgent activism at least since the 1972 Gary "independent" black political convention. At the same time, as the previously quoted criticisms by the two Youngs indicate, many elected officials saw Jackson's presidential maneuvering as an impertinent attempt by the protest element to assert a brokerage position through the electoral realm. In this sense their reaction to Jackson had the markings of a turf dispute.

Among many Jackson supporters, however, the campaign appeared to offer possibilities for overcoming internal intraelite dynamics. To the extent that they opted for a narrowly self-interested, instrumental agenda, both wings of the black political elite found themselves completely out of strategic political ideas and, even as they tried to close ranks before the Reagan onslaught, were incapable of fashioning a coherent program of racial action. The "leadership family" attempt and incessant appeals for unity reflected intraelite concern over this situation, and the failure of these efforts is instructive. Afro-American politics has been structured persistently around a client relation that binds black elites individually and primarily to external sources of patronage while they simultaneously require legitimation internally among blacks. Various attempts to institutionalize a basis for independent elite activity have unraveled before this dual accountability structure during the twentieth century. The most recent of these—the 1972 Gary initiative—demonstrated that no ideological force exists within the black community that is strong enough to take precedence over client linkages.

An often repeated lament since the early 1970s within black political circles is that, since King's assassination, blacks have suffered from the absence of an entity capable of galvanizing unity of purpose and action. Especially after the Jackson campaign picked up momentum in the media, which proclaimed the authenticity of the candidate's assertions of a mass base, several black political spokesmen raised the possibility that the "Rainbow" phenomenon could become an umbrella under which the different leadership components could be united. Robert Smith and Joseph McCormick II, two political scientists at Howard University, contended that Jackson's candidacy could "lay the organizational and financial base for the future construction of an on-going independent Black political base in national politics."[18] Roger Wilkins, unmindful of his earlier contrary view, virtually anointed Jackson as the prime mover in Afro-American political life in claiming that he already had forged a unity not seen since King and asserting that "giving respect to Jackson is symbolically giving respect to all blacks."[19]

The curious notion that Jackson represented a transcendent "moral force" in American politics might be seen in this sense as a device to justify an insurgent political campaign that was devoid of viable positions on public policy issues. Jackson's paramountcy was also seen as the long-awaited ideological symbol around which the diverse leadership elements could unite. But this symbol's attractiveness consisted mainly in its lack of concrete substance.

Moral leadership constitutes no challenge to the status claims of either elected officials or their civil rights counterparts, because it has no categorical meaning in the political world. At most, the notion that Jackson held twenty-two million moral proxies provided a convenient, temporary cover under which individual elites could push their specific agendas. Once the media-inspired elan waned, the old contradictions and tensions would inevitably reassert themselves, and the various elites would demonstrate yet again that in the world of "hardball," porkbarrel politics they inhabit, immediate material interest comes first, last, and at all points in between. Political vision lives only as a distorted mutation, and then not for long.

2

The Jackson Candidacy
and Electoral Mobilization

Intraelite conflict and strategic bankruptcy provide the backdrop for an assessment of the claims advanced by the Jackson forces. These can be distilled to six core assertions: (1) that Jackson has a base among the "black masses," who supported his efforts over elite opposition; (2) that he is a central figure in black politics in the South, a region in which he has not lived in more than a decade; (3) that a Jackson campaign was crucial for stimulating black voter registration and turnout, especially in the South; (4) that Jackson's candidacy would generate significant coattail effects, assisting the election of black candidates at state and local levels; (5) that Jackson's efforts would reinvigorate politics among Afro-Americans and stimulate political discourse in the black community; and (6) that the campaign opened the possibility for a new, progressive alliance in the Democratic party, the "Rainbow Coalition.'' The first four of these are empirical and can be considered directly.

Faced with considerable opposition from entrenched political elites in the black community, Jackson had to find some other basis through which to legitimize a candidacy that had been on his mind for years.[1] Thus originated a round of highly publicized speeches in packed black churches and auditoriums, primarily through the South. The mass media—uncaring or, as a colleague suggested, unable to distinguish between a social movement and a group of people shouting in a church—projected this Jackson tour with a sensationalism similar to that later accorded Michael Jackson. Soon a line was set; despite lackluster response from elite blacks, it was held, Jackson's initiative had overwhelming support at the ''grass roots.'' Gradually, black politicians—doubtless made insecure by their ineffectuality in the face of the general deterioration of the quality of their constituents' lives—climbed onto the campaign bandwagon. A groundswell was created with mirrors as the mass media colluded in reducing the terms of black interest in the 1984 primary season to the status of Jackson's candidacy. Nor was the Left much of a source of critical restraint; Andrew Kopkind, for example, enthusiastically and without reservation repeated the line and chided others who seemed not sufficiently excited.[2] Once the campaign tacked ''progressive'' positions on Central America and disarmament onto its mystique of a black grass-roots base, most skepticism among leftists was dissolved—except, that is, for residual Zionist concern and ambivalence over charges of anti-Semitism.

The proposition that Jackson's firmest base lay with nonelite blacks does not fare especially well under close examination. The main support for this proposition, of course, is the generally high rate at which black voters—across age, gender, and income groups—cast ballots for Jackson in the presidential primaries. However, although Jackson carried the total black vote by substantial margins in nearly every primary, table 1 raises the possibility that his most solid black electoral base actually may have been among elite strata. In nine of the thirteen primaries for which data were accessible (Alabama, District of Columbia, Illinois, Indiana, Maryland, Tennessee, Texas, Pennsylvania, and Ohio), Jackson ran better among the highest black income-earning groups than he did among the lowest. In three of the thirteen (Illinois, Indiana, and the District of Columbia), his support increased steadily with increasing income. In five other states, which did not show an unambiguous pattern of increasing Jackson support with increasing income (Alabama, Maryland, Tennessee, Texas, and Ohio), the most affluent were nonetheless the most loyal to Jackson among all black voters. (When confronted with these apparently anomalous findings, Jackson supporters adduced an antipopular explanation, noting that less affluent voters were also likely to be less well educated and less politically sophisticated and thus more susceptible to both self-hatred and the duplicity of machine politicians.)[3]

Taken alone, these findings are more suggestive than indicative with regard to refutation of the campaign's claim to grounding in "grass roots" rather than elite elements in the black community. With only one exception among the thirteen primaries Jackson received impressive majorities from all income groups. Moreover, in three of the eight in which the most affluent were the most cohesive Jackson supporters, they were also no more than five percentage points more likely to vote for Jackson than were the poorest voters. When combined with other evidence, however, the arguably slight upper-income bias in Jackson's electoral constituency becomes much more significant.

Profiles of Jackson activists also undermine grass-roots imagery. Jackson's most attentive public well may have consisted in upwardly mobile and upper-income blacks who saw the initiative as a means to further individual business or po-

TABLE 1. Black Voting for Jackson in Selected 1984 Democratic Presidential Primaries, by Income Aggregates

Annual Income ($)	Ala. (%)	D.C. (%)	Ga. (%)	Ill. (%)	Ind.[a] (%)	Md.[a] (%)	N.J. (%)	N.Y. (%)	N.C. (%)	Tenn. (%)	Texas (%)	Penn. (%)	Ohio (%)
Below 12,500	53	77	62	76	70	86	89	87	83	70	81	73	81
12,500–24,999	38	80	65	80	73	82	86	89	84	86	81	82	80
25,000–34,999	61	83	60	84	84	84	88	82	80	75	81	78	78
35,000–50,000	—	93	—	86	—	76	89	81	—	89	88	—	84
Over 50,000	—	—	—	—	—	89	—	—	—	—	—	—	—

a. Compiled by CBS News only.
Source: CBS News/New York Times 1984 Election Survey.

litical careers.[4] It is this stratum of the black population, certainly, who are most given to reducing political activity to such self-congratulatory goals as quest for self-respect or creation of "positive images" or "role models" for the race. This suspicion is strengthened by the data in table 2, which indicates that Jackson delegates scored roughly equal in income and substantially higher in educational attainment relative to Mondale and Hart delegates at the Democratic national convention.

Fifty-eight percent of Jackson delegates reported annual incomes of $35,000 or more, as compared to 63 percent of those committed to Mondale and 56 percent of those pledged to Hart. Moving still farther up the income ladder did not much

TABLE 2.   Democratic Delegate Profile

Delegate Income/yr.	Income		
	Mondale (%)	Hart (%)	Jackson (%)
Less than $12,500	2	4	5
$12,500–$24,999	12	15	16
$25,000–$34,999	19	19	17
$35,000–$49,999	24	21	24
$50,000–$74,999	16	14	18
$75,000–$100,000	7	6	3
Over $100,000	8	9	5
Unspecified over $35,000	8	6	8
Refused to specify	5	5	4

Delegate Education	Education		
	Mondale (%)	Hart (%)	Jackson (%)
Less than high school	3	0	1
High school	17	4	3
Some college	20	16	15
College graduate	19	27	25
Lawyer	12	21	13
Doctor or dentist	0	1	1
Ph.D.	3	4	6
M.A.	20	19	27
Some post-graduate	5	7	7
Refused to specify	2	1	1

Source: CBS News Democratic Delegate Survey, June 1984.

alter the delegates' parity, although the Jackson cohort fell from a slim hold on second place to a close third. Twenty-six percent of Jackson's delegates reported incomes of at least $50,000; this proportion is certainly in the same ballpark with 31 percent of Mondale's and 29 percent of Hart's. In addition, more of Jackson's delegates (54 percent) reported education beyond the baccalaureate level than did Hart's (52 percent) or Mondale's (40 percent). When black/white differentials in income and educational attainment in the society in general are considered, this rough status equivalence suggests that Jackson's delegation represented a more solidly elite stratum in the black community than either Hart's or Mondale's did among whites.

Possibly most instructive, though, is the finding that in late June, as the campaign steamed toward the convention, 49 percent of all registered blacks surveyed in a *New York Times*/CBS News poll expressed support for Mondale and only 29 percent for Jackson; among those registered as Democrats, 53 percent favored Mondale against 31 percent for Jackson.[5] Moreover, the poll indicated that only 13 percent of black respondents—including 15 percent of black Jackson supporters!—shared the candidate's opposition to runoff primaries, which he had projected as his pivotal "black" issue.[6]

Even while bearing in mind the various caveats attending generalization from such polls, it is nonetheless clear that Jackson's base among blacks is both more contingent and less uniform than his advocates would have us believe.[7] Although some credence might be given to the claim that upper-status blacks are more likely to apprehend "true" black interests, that essentially antidemocratic argument suggests a model of politics that contradicts the campaign's populist legitimations. Only one framework or the other can be adopted, unless of course the upwardly mobile petit bourgeoisie defines itself alone as "the people"—a not unheard-of self-indulgence!

One might argue that support for Jackson in the primaries should be understood as symbolic action directed toward some larger purpose and is therefore distinct from the mundane issue of actual preferences in the Democratic nomination process. This point of view (the dubious formulation of "running for respect") helps to explain the contrast between the heavy majorities of black votes that Jackson received in nearly all the primaries and caucuses on the one hand and the large plurality of Mondale support among blacks expressed in the convention-eve poll on the other. However, it also begs the question of the campaign's functional significance within its immediate context of articulation, especially since the initiative's center was the candidate rather than a discrete issue agenda. The Jackson phenomenon thus figures into that context primarily as a cathartic diverson grafted onto regular political processes. This, of course, does not deny the possibility of functional justifications that transcend the 1984 candidate selection process, but it still leaves the problem of a purportedly "serious" candidacy that must defend itself by appealing to some extrinsic and, as I shall demonstrate, equally problematic objectives.

The campaign's other largely empirical claims, all of which concern mobilization effects, are very much interconnected. Jackson's centrality as a southern force implies the coattail effect, and both revolve around the proposition concerning his impact on black voter turnout. All these claims derive from the assertion of Jackson's impact on voter registration.

Table 3 indicates that the Jackson campaign's impact on black registration is at best ambiguous. Between 1980 and 1984 black voter registration in the South as a whole increased approximately 14 percent, ranging from highs of more than 37, 28, and 23 percent in Alabama, North Carolina, and Mississippi respectively to lows of 3 percent in South Carolina—Jesse Jackson's home state—and 5 percent in Virginia and Florida. By far the greatest share of that increase appears to

TABLE 3. Black Voter Registration in the South by Presidential Election Years, 1968–84

States	1968	1972	1976	1980	1984
Alabama	273,000	290,000 (6.3)	321,000 (10.7)	350,000 (9.0)	482,000 (37.7)
Arkansas	130,000	165,000 (26.9)	204,000 (23.6)	130,000 (−36.3)	155,000 (19.2)
Florida	292,000	321,000 (9.9)	410,000 (27.7)	489,000 (19.3)	517,000 (5.7)
Georgia	344,000	450,000 (30.8)	598,000 (32.9)	450,000 (−24.7)	512,000 (13.8)
Louisiana	305,000	355,000 (16.4)	421,000 (18.6)	465,000 (10.4)	535,000 (15.0)
Mississippi	251,000	268,000 (6.8)	286,000 (6.7)	330,000 (15.3)	406,000 (23.0)
No. Carolina	305,000	298,000 (−2.3)	396,000 (32.9)	440,000 (11.1)	488,000 (10.9)
So. Carolina	189,000	206,000 (9.0)	285,000 (38.3)	320,000 (12.3)	331,000 (3.4)
Tennessee	228,000	245,000 (7.4)	271,000 (10.6)	300,000 (10.7)	348,000 (16)
Texas	540,000	575,000 (6.5)	640,000 (11.3)	620,000 (−3.1)	720,000 (16.1)
Virginia	255,000	275,000 (7.8)	317,000 (15.3)	360,000 (13.6)	378,000 (5)
Total	3,112,000	3,488,000 (12.1)	4,149,000 (18.9)	4,254,000 (2.5)	4,872,000 (14.5)

Note: Numbers in parentheses represent the percentage of increase over the previous presidential election year.
Source: Compiled from Voter Education Project, "Black Voter Registration in the South, 1940–1982," and Cavanagh and Foster, "Jesse Jackson's Campaign."

have occurred after 1982, a point which seems to buttress the campaign's claims to influence.[8] Imputation of the magnitude of that influence, however, is limited by the following factors.

First, a steady pattern of growth in black registration has been recorded in the South throughout the 1970s and 1980s, and much of the increase since 1980 can reasonably be assumed to represent continuation of that trend.[9] Second, of the states experiencing the greatest increases, two (Alabama and Mississippi) had major gubernatorial and other state races after 1982 that both preceded the Jackson initiative and occasioned substantial black mobilization;[10] in the third (North Carolina) there was considerable local mobilization after 1982 directed toward the 1984 Senate race against Jesse Helms.

Third, the apparent concentration of the black electorate's growth in the post-1982 period may be deceptive, since the relative inactivity that appears between 1980 and 1982 conceals systematic purges of voter rolls after the 1980 presidential election.[11] Fourth, the period since 1980 has witnessed a variety of intensive registration efforts conducted across the region by a number of locally and nationally based groups;[12] while the Jackson candidacy can be assumed to have enhanced those preexistent efforts, it can be assumed also to have ridden on their backs. Although the two views are not mutually exclusive, the latter may in fact weigh more heavily, since Jackson's campaign *followed* highly charged state races in a number of states recording highest increases and also had no already embedded organizational infrastructure of its own in the region.

Fifth, black people as individual citizens in the South and elsewhere are acutely conscious of suffering under the Reagan administration, and some measure of the increase in voter registration beyond "natural" growth represents—apart from any organizational impetus—the autonomous determination of black citizens to oppose that regime.

Assignment of relative weights among the "Jackson factor" and the other five would be difficult in any event. Perhaps detailed comparative examination of efforts and outcomes in individual districts could yield some tentative conclusions. However, none has been conducted to this point, and in their absence the most that can be said is that the Jackson candidacy was one element among several that stimulated black registration. Furthermore, the combined force of the more highly structured, more indigenous roots of the other organizational factors and the fact that Jackson's campaign directly supported few registration efforts under its own auspices strengthens an intuition that the "Jackson factor" alone may not have contributed very much to the surge in registration.[13]

The campaign's claims of impact on the turnout in the presidential primaries are much more plausible. In each of the primary states with considerable black populations, 1984 turnout rates were remarkably higher in black areas than in 1980, with increases of up to 87 percent in Alabama and 127 percent in New York.[14] Although the influence of the other factors that stimulated registration increases should not be ignored, there can be little doubt that the Jackson candidacy was a major precipitant of these dramatic increases. To the extent, however, that the high turnouts were a specific response to the Jackson initiative, it is not clear what their significance is for black voting in elections other than those individual primaries.

Figure 1 and table 4 provide something of an orienting context for consideration of the Jackson campaign's impact on black turnout. Both show that between the 1980 and 1984 presidential elections the gap separating white and black turnout rates narrowed by nearly 50 percent, an observation which has been duly noted by all manner of pundits and which superficially might be seen as an expression of the work of a Jackson factor. However, the relation of black to white turnout over the twenty years ending in 1984 discloses two im-

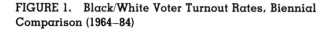

FIGURE 1. Black/White Voter Turnout Rates, Biennial Comparison (1964–84)

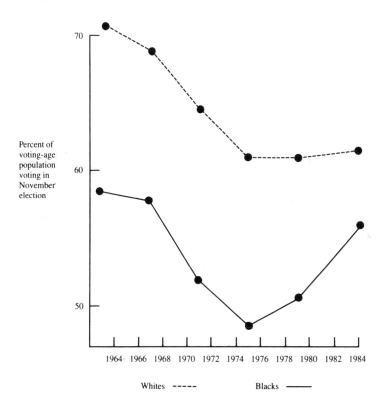

TABLE 4. Black/White Voter Turnout Rates, Biennial Comparison, 1964–84

Percentage of Voting-Age Population Voting in November Election										
Turnout	1964	1966	1968	1970	1972	1974	1976	1978	1980	1982	1984
White	70.7	57.0	69.1	56.0	64.5	46.3	60.9	47.3	60.9	49.1	61.4
Black	58.5	41.7	57.6	43.5	52.1	33.8	48.7	37.2	50.5	43.0	55.8
	12.2	16.3	11.5	12.5	12.4	12.5	12.2	10.1	10.4	6.9	5.6

Source: *Voting: Registration in the Election of 1984* (advance report), Current Population Reports Series P-20, no. 390, January 1985 (table A).

portant qualifications of any such view. First, the gap has been narrowing steadily since 1976; and, second, the most dramatic change since implementation of the Voting Rights Act occurred between 1980 and 1982. Again, as with the surge in registration, the Jackson initiative may have to take a back seat to institutionalized, ongoing mobilization efforts and independent dissatisfaction with Reaganism as a factor in increasing black voting.

Throughout the campaign the Jackson forces contended that a by-product of their efforts would be election of blacks to congressional, mayoral, and other local offices. This proposition has met empirical tests in a number of significant races; the results are not generally affirmative. On the day that Jackson ran well in the North Carolina primary, Kenneth Spaulding failed to unseat a white incumbent in that state's second congressional district, which is more than 36 percent black; on the same day, Katie Hall lost the seat to which she had been appointed in Indiana's first congressional district. Both candidates had Jackson's support, and both had been forecast with good chances to win. Although Hall's district is less than 30 percent black, her chances were considered good because she ran against two white challengers.[15] Both Spaulding and Hall ran better than Jackson in their districts. Spaulding received 48.3 percent of the vote in his district (57,684 votes) compared to Jackson's 42 percent (50,346 votes). Hall received 32.6 percent (42,345 votes) in her district where Jackson garnered 23 percent (29,245 votes).[16]

On the same day as the New Jersey primary, a black minister and Jackson advocate, Arthur Jones, failed to unseat Peter Rodino in the Newark-centered, predominantly black tenth district which Jackson carried impressively. In Georgia's 60 percent black fifth district—which Jackson had "won" handily in the Georgia primary—Atlanta Jackson activist Hosea Williams lost in August to a white incumbent. Selma, Alabama, failed in July to elect black candidates for mayor and council president over white incumbents although the municipal electorate is predominantly black and had elected its first black state senator in 1982. Later, Simeon Golar, a black challenger endorsed and actively campaigned for by Jackson, lost to white incumbent Joseph Addabo by a better than two-to-one margin in New York's sixth district in Queens, even though Jackson recently had carried the district with 63 percent of the vote in the New York presidential primary.

These failures by themselves do not completely refute the claims to coattail and transference effects. In Alabama, for example, the dramatic loss in Selma was accompanied by new black victories in smaller towns and counties.[17] Also, Robert Clark and Kenneth Moseley, black challengers for congressional seats in Mississippi and South Carolina respectively, both won in Democratic primaries (though both were defeated in general elections), and blacks won the mayoralty and a majority of council seats in Portsmouth, Virginia. All of these successful candidates credited the Jackson impetus with assisting their efforts. At least in Mississippi and South Carolina, however, the candidacies well preceded Jackson's and had generated their own well-organized local apparatus.[18]

It is interesting that the most notable successes occurred in states that did not hold electoral presidential primaries. This raises the possibility that Jackson's participation in the presidential race may have been more useful to local candidates when the energies it galvanized could be focused exclusively on local races. By contrast, in New Orleans's second congressional district—recently reapportioned to become predominantly black and which Jackson had carried solidly in the Louisiana primary—a well-known and highly regarded black challenger was unable to defeat a longtime white incumbent.

In any event, Hosea Williams in Atlanta and Arthur Jones in Newark were not generally endorsed by local black politicians, and Jackson actively campaigned for neither. Golar, like Jones, ran against a well-entrenched incumbent with a very liberal record. Indeed, in each case defeat can be explained by peculiarities of local politics. Every local race is dominated by its own mitigating circumstances. This explanation hardly strengthens the transference proposition. Rather, it discloses what sensitivity to the character of American electoral politics would have indicated all along, that the determinants of outcomes in local elections are manifold and complex, and that the concatenations of interests, cleavages, and coalitions operative within the individual jurisdictions bear heavily on electoral success. The influence of a "Jackson factor" thus depends on the existence of a constellation of local forces that already favors electoral success. In addition to this qualification of the transference claim, the Jackson phenomenon has stimulated two dynamics that might negatively affect electoral outcomes. Outside the black community the campaign may have fueled a white countermobilization; inside, it has introduced a new line of political cleavage that already has manifested itself in electoral conflict.

Although campaign rhetoric made a great deal of Jackson's "carrying" states, cities, and congressional districts in the primaries, much of that success was the function not only of massive black turnouts but also of equally significant white nonvoting. In a Southern Regional Council study of voting patterns in targeted precincts, more than half of the predominantly white precincts reported participation of less than 30 percent in the Alabama, Georgia, and Florida primaries.[19] Jackson's impressive victory in Louisiana was made possible by record low white voting,[20] and Tennessee's primary lured only 10 percent of white voters.[21] In every primary state except Illinois, the large black turnout increases over 1980 far outstripped state totals and in Pennsylvania and Georgia were accompanied by actual statewide decline.[22] In Massachusetts and New Hampshire—states with very small black populations—a pattern of significant decline from 1980 was clear;

Rhode Island experienced a slight increase from 1980, but the level of voting there was substantially down from 1976.[23] Low rates of white voting in Democratic primaries cannot be attributed simply to a backlash against Jackson. It is at least equally likely that they indicate prior commitment to Reagan or general dissatisfaction with existing Democratic options. At a minimum, though, low white participation limits the significance of the campaign's apparent mobilization effects and further qualifies projection of transference effects.

At the same time, the possibility that some element of white disaffection does reflect anti-Jackson backlash raises the prospect of a white countermobilization. An official of the National Republican Congressional Committee boasted that Jackson was "driving white voters into the Republican Party," especially in the South.[24] In general, Republicans seemed tolerant, if not supportive, of Jackson's initiative.[25] While this posture might be seen as whistling past the graveyard, wishful thinking, or a desire to avoid further antagonizing of blacks, Jesse Helms, among the Republicans involved in tightly contested campaigns, definitely sought to create a countermobilization by identifying his opponent with Jackson.[26]

Less partisan sources also have noted the possibility of countermobilization. Cavanagh and Foster raise the specter of this reaction in their report on the Jackson campaign,[27] and a later survey conducted by Gallup for the Joint Center for Political Studies found that 17 percent of white respondents nationally said that they were less likely to vote for Mondale because of Jackson's endorsement, compared to 10 percent who said they were more likely.[28] At any rate, table 5 indicates that the net effect of the furious and racially polarized mobilization and countermobilization in the South was at best (from the standpoint of black interests) a washout.

Perhaps most instructive is the response of South Carolina Jackson advocates to the candidate's short-lived intention to contend for Strom Thurmond's U.S. Senate seat in that state. The South Carolina director of Jackson's campaign initially refused even to take the proposed senate race seriously. Another prominent Jackson activist in Columbia judged the proposed candidacy "counterproductive," explicitly citing fear that Jackson's entry would incite white opposition.[29] Although any highly publicized black candidacy probably would generate backlash, this tendency is exacerbated by Jackson activists' disposition to articulate electoral goals in exclusively—often crudely—racial terms, "Rainbow" slogans notwithstanding.[30]

TABLE 5. Racial Composition of Southern Presidential Vote, 1980 and 1984

	1980 (%)	1984 (%)
White	86	87
Black	12	11
Other	2	2

Source: ABC News Poll, "Yearend Wrapup."

The campaign's local mobilization effects may be limited also—in the short term, at least—by an unanticipated product of the adversarial climate that it has fostered in the black community. Putting aside rhetorical claims to a "mass" base, anecdotal evidence indicates that the Jackson phenomenon nonetheless acted as a catalyst for politicians who perceived their aspirations blocked by entrenched political elites in the black community. Although the black Alabama Democratic Conference endorsed Mondale in the primary, the *Washington Post* reported that Jackson had much of the support of "younger, less well-known office-holders."[31] Similar situations occurred in Georgia (where Coretta Scott King, Andrew

Young, and Julian Bond supported Mondale) and elsewhere. The ensuing version of "two-line struggle"—conducted under a rubric of claims to authenticity of racial leadership, with loyalty to the Jackson effort as the litmus test—seems to have animated tensions within elite circles, fueling assaults by aspiring claimants against entrenched spokesmen. This conflict was illustrated in the Jackson delegates' booing of King and Young at the Democratic convention.[32]

Early in the campaign Jackson activists in Chicago threatened to oppose Mayor Harold Washington's reelection because of his reluctance to endorse their candidate.[33] Julian Bond—whose lackadaisical record in the state legislature increased his vulnerability—faced stiff opposition from a habitual, unsuccessful candidate for various offices in Atlanta who enhanced his credibility by running under the Jackson flag.[34] Arthur Jones and Hosea Williams in their congressional races ran against white incumbents supported by their districts' black elites. In Mississippi a black Jackson activist, previously unsuccessful in attempts to win local office, threatened to enter a U.S. senate race as an independent in defiance of the state's black Democratic leadership's endorsement of a white contender against the Reaganite incumbent. A black state senate candidate in South Carolina, a Mondale convention delegate, found indifference to his campaign from Jackson supporters.[35] These instances suggest that the element of the Jackson initiative that is rooted in intraelite competition may—until new relationships are adjusted—increase black electoral conflict, thus raising the possibility of voter demoralization and fragmentation. Without the protection of some mechanism like the runoff primary such conflict could diminish the likelihood of electoral success, particularly in near or slim black majority districts. Although increased electoral competition ultimately might serve democratic purposes—depending on its specific content—its immediate electoral impact could be dysfunctional. Moreover, the Jackson initiative's potential as a democratizing influence in black political activity is severely hampered, as I shall argue, by its fundation in a fundamentally antidemocratic, antiparticipatory political style in the black community. Before joining that issue, however, some remarks concerning Jackson's political centrality in the South are in order.

A mystique of the South surrounded the Jackson campaign from the beginning. The first, highly publicized Jackson tour in the summer and fall of 1983 concentrated on southern audiences, and the initial claims to mass base were grounded on the picture of acclamation by throngs in southern churches and college auditoriums. Jackson himself, of course, belongs to the interminable list of protest politicians who legitimize themselves by projecting images of association with King and the civil rights movement. This imagery was reinforced by the circumstance that the campaign's credibility depended heavily on the cluster of early primaries in southern states with large black populations. Yet Jesse Jackson has not lived in the South for more than a decade. His base of operations—to the extent that his influence inheres to any concrete terrain— is in Chicago, which only occasionally appears to be a colonial outpost of Arkansas and Mississippi.

This mystique persists because it feeds on a perception of southern black political life that is at best anachronistic. The perception rests on an assumption that the black South is a politically underdeveloped territory in which (a) political aspirations are typically expressed indirectly, through the mediation of churches and preachers, and (b) broad-scale mobilization awaits or requires the intervention of some external, extraordinary force. That assumption, which lingers from the era of systemically enforced black disfranchisement, is at this point emphatically false. While 53 percent of the Afro-American population is located in the South, the region as of 1983 accounted for 61 percent of all black elected officials.[36] The three largest cities in the Deep South—Atlanta, New Orleans, and Birmingham—all have black mayors and solidly entrenched political organizations. The rate of increase in black officeholding between 1970 and 1982 was at least twice as high in the South as in any other region.[37]

Moreover, 67 percent of all black officeholders nationally serve in jurisdictions of 50,000 or fewer constituents,[38] and, given that the South's population density is lower than in the other areas of significant black officeholding,[39] it is reasonable to assume that this national percentage is at least matched in that region. The same assumption holds for the functional distribution of officials. The Joint Center for Political Studies reports that in 1980 8.6 percent of black officials held county office, 48.3 percent municipal office (36.8 percent council members), 10.6 percent judicial or law enforcement office, and 24.9 percent educational office (23.6 percent on local school boards).[40] The existence of numerous predominantly black southern counties strongly implies greater than proportionate southern composition at that level, including the judicial/law enforcement category. The black South, therefore, hardly appears to be deficient in official linkage mechanisms or indigenous political leadership, at least not in relation to other regions.

Thus, a persisting erroneous perception of the black South and the continually problematic character of "black leadership" as an analytic and political category conceal the nakedness of assertions of Jackson's southern empire. Because the nature of Jackson's leadership status lies outside the realm of palpable constituencies of discrete individuals, it can be projected without constraint by requirements of validation. Because discussion of Afro-American affairs is so often dominated by a patronizing, exceptionalist bias that suspends norms of critical reflection and judgment, intrinsically absurd claims frequently attain currency. Imagine Tom Hayden, for example, claiming the Midwest as his current organizational base on the strength of having lived and worked there twenty years ago!

Regarding the actual substance of the centrality of Jackson's influence in the South, three instances speak eloquently. First, the rate of increase in black voter registration between 1980 and 1984 in South Carolina, Jackson's home state, was easily the lowest in the region. Second, his aborted plan to enter the South Carolina U.S. Senate race was opposed as counterproductive even by indigenous Jackson supporters. Third, in the aftermath of the city's 1980 civil disturbance, Jackson traveled to Miami, as did Andrew Young, to present himself as mediator and broker of the black community's interests. This arrogated status claim was rejected emphatically; both men were hooted and denounced at community meetings as uninvited, impertinent outsiders. Combined with the ambiguity surrounding Jackson's claims to inspire registration and to generate support for local initiatives, these instances underscore the inherent illogicality of the notion of his centrality in the South.

So was MLK Jr in White + Chgr, so what?

3

The Jackson Phenomenon
and Leadership Ratification

n light of our assessment of the campaign's empirical claims two questions loom: (1) Why was the Jackson initiative able to dominate Afro-American politics through the presidential nomination season? (2) What is its significance beyond its faulty projections of short-term electoral impact? The answers to both questions lie in situating the Jackson phenomenon in relation to models of leadership and political style in the black community. Therein also lies the path to assessing one of the Jackson advocates' major nonempirical claims, that is, that the campaign revitalized politics among Afro-Americans.

As I have argued, the developing tension between black protest elites and electoral political elites reflects both competition for occupation of race leadership niches and conflicting principles of legitimation. From Booker T. Washington's well-known 1895 speech and his ensuing controversy with

31

W. E. B. DuBois and other advocates of racial protest until passage of the 1965 Voting Rights Act, articulation of black leadership was characterized by a largely unrecognized anomaly. During that period, over which a national leadership stratum solidified, verifiable mechanisms for validating leadership claims were practically nonexistent in the black community. Blacks in the South, where the population was concentrated, were systematically excluded from voting, and in northern and midwestern cities gerrymandering and other obstacles placed fetters on electoral impact that were overcome only gradually and sporadically. In the absence of effective external support for change, the inaccessibility of electoral legitimations was simply a given element of black leadership and required elaboration of alternative strategies both for defining and pressing racial agendas and for authenticating claims to spokesmanship status.

This situation produced two results. First, there was an institutionalization of extraelectoral protest politics, typified in the NAACP's strategy that focused on fighting racial exclusion through the courts. Second, there emerged a distinctive pattern of dual leadership validation.

In a context that since the 1890s had assumed the political muteness of the black community, entrenched white elites, through a monopoly over political resources required by black leaders, functioned as arbiters for aspirants to spokesmanship status among Afro-Americans.[1] This situation, in its turn, forced black aspirants for leadership to base their claims on grounds of racial authenticity (that is, on group-primalistic grounds), lacking as they did the concrete resources and institutional mechanisms for basing leadership claims on more functional or secular grounds. Thus Afro-American politics, both North and South (mainly for small urban enclaves until the 1960s), would be characterized in the twentieth century by a charismatic model of political authority and a corollary, intransigent assumption of black attitudinal uniformity.[2] Both

carry rather problematic normative and practical ramifications, which become more visible as this paradigm of organic
or primalist leadership legitimation is carried forth into the
1970s and 1980s.

The most immediate practical difficulty posed now by the
principle of organic legitimation concerns the rise of a competing principle in the post–Voting Rights era. Although
electoral and protest elites equally incline toward securing black
loyalties through appeals to organic racial collectivity, the
former ultimately must meet the requirements of more for-
mally articulated legitimating rules. As a consequence, on the
one hand, electoral elites are constrained in their claims to
represent black interests in ways that protest politicians are
not. Electorally based claims are limited ultimately by jurisdictional boundaries and are subject to procedurally inscribed
public affirmation at regular intervals. On the other hand,
elected officials' claims to authenticity rest on less uncertain,
albeit narrower, ground. While there is considerable room for
disputation of Coleman Young's assertion that big-city mayors are the proper repositories of collective Afro-American
aspirations, his status as a spokesman for black political interests in Detroit—so long as he is returned to office—is institutionalized in the political system and is beyond question.
No protest politician can adduce such conclusive evidence of
popular affirmation.

What I have just described, of course, are very rudimentary characteristics of representative democracy; it is necessary to belabor them only because they generally have not
figured into consideration of the category of "black leadership." However, one dimension of the current tension between electoral and protest elites is that the former—through
little fault of their own—have introduced formal democratic
representation as an alternative to organicism for the first time
in the black community since Reconstruction.

In this sense the Jackson phenomenon might be seen as an

attempt to assert organic legitimation claims through the instrumental domain of electoral politics. That view underscores the soundness of those observers who heard in Jackson's campaign resonant echoes of the electoral populism
characterized by George Wallace in 1968 and 1972[3]—and,
for that matter, by Jimmy Carter in 1976, Reagan in 1980,
and the New Right in general. Jackson, like Wallace and the
others, presented himself as an embodiment of collectively held
values rather than as the representative of an instrumental issue agenda; his claim to authenticity derived from his assertion of a direct relation to a mass constituency—a relation that
was presumed to exist outside of and prior to formal political
linkages. His campaign to that extent sought to use electoral
mechanisms, which are essentially formal and procedural, to
validate a leadership relation that is essentially antiformal and
antiprocedural.

An irony of this political style, and the leadership model
in which it is embedded, is that—while ostensibly popular and
immediately representative—it is fundamentally antidemocratic. Antiformalism leaves acclamation as the sole principle
of popular validation. However, only at rare moments of
widespread popular mobilization, during active, self-regener-
ative social movements, is this acclamation accessible to public verification. Only in such instances does the mass constituency constitute a discursive community that can steer and
discipline leadership. Otherwise, without palpable mechanisms of ratification, no evidentiary base exists from which
to determine veracity of leadership claims; nor is there any
way for an amorphous, posited constituency to affirm or reject claimants' actions.

In the Afro-American context the antidemocratic character
of the organic leadership style has been obscured by the primacy of external linkages to white elites. Protest leadership
is beset by the contradiction that certification of its authenticity normally is attained outside the black community.[4] Never-

theless, that leadership status rests on a premise of unmediated representation of a uniform racial totality, and this premise has fostered a model of political authority that is antidiscursive and deemphasizes popular accountability. As this model descends from the realm of interelite negotiation to popular politics, it discloses a hortatory and charismatic aspect which—in the absence of restraints imposed by electoral formalism or a self-propelling, goal-oriented political movement—tends naturally toward authoritarianism.

The organic relation, in the course of eliminating instrumental distinctions between leadership and constituents, also eliminates accountability and—by extension—the principle of representation. Commitment to this organic view, by assuming complete identity of racial interests, inhibits the constituency from participating in the rational articulation of political goals. Thus, the fortunes and preferences of constituents simply are collapsed into those of leadership. No arena exists for debate of the subjectively defined objectives of leadership. Loyalty, then, becomes less a function of adherence to a popular issue agenda than an expression of obedience to leadership's arbitrary definitions of the requirements of the posited racial totality. Because the objectives of leadership and the interests of the constituents are presumed identical, dissent is tantamount to treason.

This logic organizes the leadership style of protest politics in the black community, and its coordinates underlie the Jackson phenomenon. Jackson's initiative was not so much a political campaign as a crusade. Jackson himself acknowledged early that his effort was concerned less with specific political issues than with forging an identity with his claimed constituency, an identity based on "trust" and "the ability to inspire through qualities of leadership."[5] Although this kind of manufactured image is now common coin in presidential campaigns—with Reagan perhaps the most adroit trader ever—Jackson went further. He compared himself to Jackie Robinson in carrying "the emotions and self-respect and inner security of the whole race."[6] His advisers did not initiate discussions leading to formulation of an issue agenda until May 1984.[7] Astoundingly, as the campaign wheeled toward the Democratic convention, not only was there no indication of what issues the candidate would press regarding platform or policy, but the fact that Jackson planned to contend in the name of the entire Afro-American population for a bill of particulars that was completely unknown—even among Jackson supporters—a month before the convention generated little criticism or concern.[8] The Jackson platform finally constructed was jerry-built and collapsed at the convention ultimately because it had no popular foundation.

If revitalization of politics is taken to mean stimulation of interest in and debate of public policy alternatives that confront the black community, then the Jackson candidacy's claims in that regard have no basis. Indeed, by fomenting a climate that disqualified all issues other than unquestioning support of Jackson, the campaign effectively stifled black political discourse. Skepticism and disagreement were vilified by the Jackson camp as racial heresy. The chairman of the Alabama Democratic Conference complained that Jackson supporters castigated blacks associated with Mondale as "Uncle Toms."[9] A black minister in Birmingham asserted that blacks who did not support Jackson "should be ashamed of themselves."[10] The *Washington Post* reporter who disclosed Jackson's infamous "Hymie town" remarks was roundly denounced as a Judas, not only by Louis Farrakhan but by Jackson supporters generally.[11] These examples only capture a flavor of the conformism that the campaign demanded of the black population. Reasoned debate was incompatible with and intolerable to the spirit of self-righteous crusade with which Jackson's candidacy was imbued.

In fact, the campaign traded on a politics of expressive catharsis that is antirational at its core. I recall a late-night dis-

cussion of the campaign's efficacy with two Jackson supporters—one a college-educated campaign coordinator—on a street
corner in New Haven's black community. The encounter
quickly deteriorated, with one of the Jackson advocates
screaming that if all eligible blacks registered and voted,
Jackson could win the presidency—citing the oft-mentioned
census undercount of blacks as a conspiratorial ploy to conceal the fact of a black majority in the United States.[12] A
woman in New Orleans walked for an hour and a half to take
her family to ''see a President''; when restrained by Secret
Service agents, she complained, ''All I wanted to do is just
touch him.''[13] Jackson cultivated this cathartic disposition with
tent-revivalist imagery. He told of a terminally ill Virginia
supporter who insisted on leaving his hospital bed to attend a
campaign rally at which his condition improved so dramati-
cally that his doctor ordered new tests, only to find no evidence of his earlier cancer.[14] Always given to drape himself
in the cultural authority of King's image, Jackson thus as-
sessed his success in the New York primary: ''What was a
crucifixion in April of 1968 [became] a resurrection in April
of 1984.''[15] The message is clear: the campaign's mission was
divinely inspired. Only apostates could refuse to accept it on
its own terms.

   These are but a small sample of instances that illustrate the
extent to which the Jackson phenomenon reduced Afro-
American participation in the 1984 presidential selection process to a depoliticized, cathartic zeal. Behind the superficial
appearances of Jackson's charisma and oratory and the rhetorical claims about instilling hope and generating motion, there
lies a quite different reality. The hope that Jackson preached
was not grounded in politics; if it were, its themes would have
centered around concrete, strategic options. Instead, the campaign manipulated its adherents' fears and despair in much
the same way as do the quick-fix purveyors of lucky rabbits'
feet, millenarian cults, and religions of positive thinking.

Jackson's initiative not only diverted Afro-American attention from the dynamic of secular political debate that is the heart of democracy; the campaign actively sought to reconstitute politics in the black community as a conceptually empty, self-aggrandizing zealotry.

A predictable "pragmatic" defense against this interpretation takes one of two forms: either that Jackson gave his constituents what they wanted or that black mobilization requires pandering to catharsis. Response to the first is simple. What people want is conditioned by their perceptions of the options available to them. Jackson's success in securing identification with his effort, therefore, reflects not only his adeptness at tapping reservoirs of emotion in the black community and enforcing an authoritarian demand for unity that suppresses the right to disagree within the race. It also implicates the general failure of black political elites to formulate programmatic agendas that are meaningful to their claimed constituents in the contemporary political situation.

Two problems confront the second form of this defense. First, it is questionable empirically. The history of at least the past three decades provides numerous examples of popularly based, purposive black political activity, both electoral and nonelectoral. The community action movement spawned sophisticated organizational elaborations, such as the National Welfare Rights Organization and the National Tenants' Organization, which functioned as rational interest groups. Locally, legions of poor people's organizations, community and neighborhood associations, and ad-hoc civil rights groups have demonstrated the viability of purposively rational political action among Afro-Americans. Moreover, the growth of black elected officialdom in the 1970s and 1980s has been based practically on instrumental political organization; the Jackson campaign's electoral success appears to have been largely a function of support from this entrenched organizational base. Certainly, mobilization of emotional commitment and collec-

tive vision are required to maintain concerted action, especially among people whose principal political resource is personal energy. However, that energy has been marshalled just
as easily in service to goal-oriented, instrumental activity as
it has been mobilized for catharsis.

The second problem with this defense concerns the proper
functions of those who present themselves as political leaders. For even if we assume the black population to be particularly susceptible to charismatic mobilization—if only because it is inherited and familiar—we must then ask whether
responsible leadership should pander to an antirational, overly
simple political style simply because it is driven by cultural
inertia and is therefore convenient. Should not leadership—
most of all leadership that bases its claims on moral authority—strive to inspire constituents to transcend those of their
practices and dispositions which undermine the democratic
values of autonomy and open community and which leave them
ill-equipped to face the challenges that confront them as citizens? How should we judge the claims of a putative leadership that, like market research-based television programming,
deliberately offers nothing that might stimulate an unpredict-
able reaction in those who are led?

Such questions seldom arise with regard to the black charismatic style. Nor is their absence simply a theoretical over-
sight. A premise of Afro-American exceptionalism, which
originated in its current guise in black power ideology in the
late 1960s, insists that norms concerning the formal characteristics of democratic polity and citizenship do not apply directly among black Americans. Divorced from its radically
separatist elaborations, this premise demands exemption of
black political elites from judgment on the basis of behavioral
criteria associated with a wide variety of these norms, for example, conflict of interest, nepotism, and other injunctions
concerning public ethics. The more remote values of rational
discourse and democratic participation do not even surface as

possible sanctions governing behavior within the black community. This puts black elites in the curious position of justifying their demands for collective representation in the pluralist distributive queue through appeals to norms of fair play, equality, and participation, while substantively denying the propriety of those norms within the black population. Reliance on an expressive politics within the black community helps to conceal this fundamental contradiction.

4

Mythology of the Church in Contemporary Afro-American Politics

Exceptionalist approaches to black politics typically are fed by the mystique of black churchliness and religiosity, which postulates a peculiarly racial basis of participation and representation. According to this view, which assumes the organic leadership model, the church is the elemental unit of political mobilization in the black community. Because its structures are decentralized and operate at the "grass roots," the black church can be construed as an authentically popular institution. Moreover, because this view also assumes a pandemic black religiosity, the church can be understood to be prior and superior to electoral or otherwise procedural institutions as a source of popular legitimations.

41

The Mystique of the Black Church and the Jackson Campaign

The mystique of the black church suffused the Jackson campaign. Among its various entailments, Jackson's candidacy was accompanied by—if not founded upon—reassertion of both ministerial claims to primary black leadership status and notions of the centrality of the church as a political linkage institution and agency for popular mobilization. Jackson's early attempts to circumvent entrenched elites proceeded from his definition of the church as a terrain for effective mass validation. A religious metaphor dominated the campaign and gave credence to efforts by church spokesmen to project the image of their organic authority into electoral politics.

Not only did Jackson go to churches to legitimize his intention to run; his initiative consistently fused religion and politics. During his instructively labeled "Southern Crusade" the potential candidate entreated crowds to submit to a "voter registration character oath," sworn on the Bible and enlisting God on his behalf.[1] Even in New Hampshire Jackson conducted campaign rallies like revival meetings—to the point of isolating groups of unregistered sinners before the gathering, signing up volunteers on the spot in a spirit of testimony and conversion, and calling forth public pledges in a descending series of specified dollar amounts.[2] Strong implications of divine mission underlay his claim to embody a "moral force" in the campaign, and his widely acclaimed oratorical performance at the Democratic convention abounded with references to God in general and Christ in particular.[3] Speaking at the Congressional Black Caucus Legislative Weekend a month before the 1984 presidential election, Jackson—in his campaign hero role—forthrightly lauded the fusion of politics and religion in the black community.[4]

Although church linkages have long been considered important mechanisms for turning out black voters,[5] the Jackson campaign seems to have encouraged ministerial inclinations toward direct involvement in politics in black communities. Arthur Jones, the Methodist pastor who contested in Rodino's congressional district, had never before stood for political office.[6] In the District of Columbia and Maryland—as elsewhere—ministerial alliances constituted the most energetic organizational support base for the campaign and pledged to transfer that involvement to their local political arenas.[7] In Alabama, Jackson advocate C. T. Vivian, a minister and civil rights movement veteran, proclaimed that "the greatest communicator in America is the black preacher" and alleged ministerial authority to be the foundation of black political activism.[8]

The Context of the Black Church's Political Involvement

Electoral involvement by black ministry is not a novel phenomenon; Adam Clayton Powell, Jr., whose lengthy congressional career was supported by his pastorate of Harlem's Abyssinian Baptist Church, exemplifies the common nexus of church and politics. Philadelphia's congressman William Gray III, Andrew Young, and Walter Fauntroy attest to the continuing significance of ministerial background among black elected officials. However, the development of a new context of political authority in the aftermath of the civil rights movement had deemphasized the church's role in political spokesmanship. Kilson notes that profiles of elected officials since 1965 reveal typical occupational backgrounds in secular professions, for example, law, teaching, and engineering.[9] In Atlanta, the growth of a stratum of black elected officials eliminated the political functions of the largely church-based leadership of the 1950s and 1960s, and there is no reason to believe the process unique to that city.[10] By the 1980s,

DuBois's 1903 prediction of the supersession of a clerically grounded leadership appeared to have reached fruition.[11] The Jackson phenomenon in this respect represents a resurgence of the principle of clerical political spokesmanship.

This principle derives its legitimations directly from the mythology surrounding the black church. The functions that it has performed historically in the black community yield an impression of the church as the principal linkage institution in Afro-American life. Empirical evidence of the black community's reliance on church networks in mobilizing for collective action corroborates this view and extends perception of the priority of religious institutions into the political domain. However, this interpretation does not account for several characteristics of the twentieth-century church's functions that explicitly have impinged on politics in ways that suggest a far more ambiguous relation between the two.

Aldon D. Morris, in a major sociological study of the institutional foundations of civil rights activism between the 1953 Baton Rouge bus boycott and the sit-ins, succumbs to the folly of confounding the church's significance as a terrain for mobilization with the altogether different claim that it was the authorizing "chief institutional force behind" activism. In making that specious inference, Morris sidesteps the need to address two problematic issues concerning his assertion of the church's political primacy: (1) the fact that the same church had existed in political quietude for two generations before the 1950s and (2) the fact that the church was by no means universally active in or supportive of civil rights protest, as I shall show later in this chapter.[12]

Regarding the notion of universality of the church's support for civil rights activism, even in the Montgomery boycott King had denounced the "apathy of the Negro ministers," as well as the quiescent model of religion propagated in the black church.[13] Later, King's indictment of the black church would become more sweeping as he charged: "Two

types of Negro churches have failed to provide bread. One
burns with emotionalism, and the other freezes with classism.
. . . The so-called Negro church has also left men disap-
pointed at midnight.'' [14]

Any rigorous analysis of the link between politics and the
black church must delineate the developmental context—and
the trajectory of actions and choices dictated by this context—through which the twentieth-century black church
evolved. First of all, the historical context was the regime of
racial segregation which, by restricting the scope of black institutional articulation, left the church as a largely unrivalled
repository for associational activity. The intrinsic link of the
church's institutional primacy and black exclusion from other
channels for social action—including, most of all, politics—
was clear to the generation of functionalist sociologists and
social psychologists who studied the Afro-American community in the 1930s and 1940s. Even though they assigned
great value to the church's integrative and stabilizing effects
on group life, E. Franklin Frazier, Charles S. Johnson, and
others recognized that those functions fell to the church by
default, as a result of the systemically (and juridically) de-
creed absence of competing institutions. Frazier indicated that
the church accommodated the expulsion of blacks from participation in the polity by creating a substitute arena in which
''the struggle for power and the thirst for power could be satisfied.'' [15] Moreover, he argued, the church provided an alternative to political participation (in the form of election of
church officers and convention delegates), and he observed
that denominational loyalty substituted for political identity. [16]
Although Johnson typically was loath to discuss the restrain-
ing context of the prevailing racial order, he nonetheless
obliquely connected the primacy of the church in the rural black
South of the 1930s with the restrictions imposed by segregation; the church's importance was associated with its status as
the ''only institution which provides an effective organization

of the group, an approved and tolerated place for social activities.''[17] He noted as well, adducing increasing education and literacy as contributing factors, that the church was less central in the lives of the youth, who were ''both more mobile and less docile'' than their elders.[18] While Frazier and, especially, Johnson were most concerned with the church's sociologically adaptive functions, the political implications of their perspectives on its foundations in the South are clear.[19] Development of the church's institutional prominence proceeded from acceptance of—as a given condition—the removal of blacks from the polity; to that extent, the avenues of expression that it opened should be seen as constituting not a parallel form of political institution or indirect means to political development, but rather a categorical *alternative* to politics as an appropriate activity in the black community.

Inasmuch as exclusion was the most salient political issue confronting Afro-Americans, the institutional force of the church must be included among the several factors that retarded political development. The church exerted anticonfrontational pressures both passively and actively. Dollard in the 1930s found that the church, in addition to cementing black social solidarity and providing individual consolation, also served as a ''mechanism for the social control of Negroes,'' as illustrated by the welcoming spirit with which planters generally greeted black church activity and its disparagements of this-worldly issues.[20] Frazier observed that organizational space existed for the black church's unique autonomous institutional elaboration because black religion ''offered no threat to the white man's dominance in both economic and social relations.''[21] He added that because of its consistently otherworldly focus, ''on the whole, the Negro's church was not a threat to white domination and aided the Negro to become accommodated to an inferior status.''[22] Davis and his coauthors, however, implicated the church as a more active agency in securing the order of racial domination. They found evidence of collusion between planters and church and lodge organizations to guarantee steady incomes for the latter through the medium of ostensible cash advances to tenants.[23] Like Dollard, they noted the ''general practice of landlords in encouraging tenants to build churches and in giving them financial aid for this purpose.'' These authors took that observation a step further and reported that black church doctrines in the 1930s characteristically incorporated the ''dogma that not the agricultural economy but [members'] own thriftlessness and sinfulness were responsible'' for their poverty.[24] Their research in general disclosed ''the operation of the dogma of the Negro rural church to strengthen . . . caste controls.''[25]

At the same time in northern cities a different situation prevailed. Frazier noted that the greater occupational differentiation experienced by blacks in cities diminished both the centrality of the church as an associational entity and the prominence of clerical leadership.[26] He observed also that the secularizing pressures of urbanization encouraged the church—at least in middle-class pastorates—toward engagement in political and social affairs.[27] Nevertheless Drake and Cayton found considerable secularly grounded disaffection with the church among Depression-era black Chicagoans.[28] In 1944, Myrdal, who continued to acknowledge its binding role, found the black church to have been ''lagging ideologically.'' He noted that in a context of growing political activism and protest the church ''remained conservative and accommodating,''[29] despite the occasional appearance of activist ministers.[30] During the 1930s, Bunche found that the church in northern cities ''occupie[d] a most important position in politics'';[31] at the same time, regarding the South, he held the black clergy largely responsible for the fact that ''more progress has not been made in bettering the social, economic, and political life of the Negro,'' noting even the urban church's typical refusal to engage political or societal issues.[32]

These reports indicate that assertions of historical connection of the church and politics among Afro-Americans require substantial qualification. Throughout the period of segregation's hegemony the church in the South functioned as a most frequently antagonistic alternative to political involvement. Outside the South, when the church ventured into politics, it followed "not a peculiarly Negro but a typical American pattern" of trading ministerial influence for primarily self-interested patronage gain.[33] In sum, the myth of the black church as the source of autonomous, popularly based political activity has scant factual basis in the first half of the twentieth century.

The Political Role of the Black Church Assessed

The myth of a politically active black church draws its immediate sustenance from more recent images associated with heroic engagement in the civil rights movement. For Walter Fauntroy, Andrew Young, Hosea Williams, Joseph Lowery, Benjamin Hooks, Ralph David Abernathy, C. T. Vivian, and others whose claims to political leadership status somehow involve ministerial or church connections—most of all, Jesse Jackson—the authority that they invoke derives not merely from the cloth, but from their association with the clerical wing of civil rights activism. Jackson, for example, in his campaign constantly cited his earlier involvement in the civil rights movement to prove himself more worthy than his opponents.[34] The ministerial resurgence accompanying his candidacy evokes identification of the church with organic bonds of protest politics that predate electoral legitimations; its resonance with the styles of civil rights struggle gives this imagery the sense of moral priority. However, even in relation to the surge of civil rights protest in the 1950s and 1960s the church's record is ambivalent.

Doug McAdam, in a recent study of the sources of black activism, acknowledges the church's social quiescence in earlier periods but finds that "the southern urban black church evidenced increased involvement in social action after about 1940."[35] From 1956—two years after the Brown decision—to 1959, McAdam's research indicates, church-based leadership in fact was pivotal in originating direct action protest activity.[36] In general during those years he finds that "indigenous leaders were overwhelmingly drawn from the ranks of black ministers, students, or local NAACP personnel."[37] In the aftermath of the Montgomery bus boycott the ministerial leadership component was most visible. Yet both before and after that period the initiative lay elsewhere. Of all movement-led actions between 1955 and 1960, church-based groups were responsible for only 12 percent; student groups, by contrast, led in 31 percent of the total.[38] Between 1961 and 1965, campus and church-based groups together accounted for only 13 percent of movement events, steadily declining to a low of 6 percent in 1965.[39] Although, as McAdam suggests, this development reflects incorporation of early church (and student) leadership into increasingly consolidated specialized organizations, King's Southern Christian Leadership Conference—the principal vehicle of clerical activism—initiated only 23 percent of movement events over the first half of the 1960s.[40]

Case study material substantiates the church's actual relationship to political leadership in the civil rights era. Burgess found in the Durham, North Carolina, of 1960 that "the minister has never been the only, or even the main, source of leadership" and that the "business and professional world has from the first been of equal, if not more, importance as a source of leadership."[41] Clerical dispositions toward social activism were divided into two clearly discernible camps—one defining intervention into "race relations" as a proper concern of the church, the other eschewing such temporal activity.[42] William Chafe's study of civil rights and black power activism in Greensboro, North Carolina, records a ministerial reluctance in the late 1950s to endorse the racial protest style associated with King, to the point that no church was willing to provide a forum for the Montgomery boycott leader's 1958 visit.[43] He describes the typical posture of the city's black clergy toward politics during the activist years as representing "the quintessence of caution."[44] In Hunter's classic 1953 study of Atlanta, of the thirty-four individuals scoring on a reputational scale as major black leaders, six were ministers, and they "were not considered top leaders in a policy-making sense by those within the leadership group itself who voted on them."[45] Black informants, furthermore, stressed the temporally active clergy's obstructionist proclivities toward reducing policy and projects to narrow self-interest.[46]

These cases do not approximate a comprehensive picture of the church's relation to civil rights protest in southern cities, and the experience of each might be taken to reflect local idiosyncrasies.[47] Thompson, by contrast, found that in black New Orleans in the early 1960s, "ministers constitute the largest segment of the leadership class,"[48] and Ladd noted the significance of clerical political spokesmanship in Winston-Salem, North Carolina, and Greenville, South Carolina, in the mid-1960s.[49] On the other hand, because the urban church was more likely to be socially and politically engaged than its rural counterpart, these cities represent a sample culled from a universe that is already biased toward clerical involvement in politics.[50] Therefore, a minimal conclusion is that the view that projects the church as the authentic source of Afro-American political action is very much an overstatement. Moreover, if there is a case that is clearly unrepresentative of general patterns in the urban South, it is New Orleans. Not only is the city—including its black population—in general culturally marginal to the South; at the time of Thompson's study at least a third of black New Orleanians and a majority of the city as a whole were Catholic. Black Protestant churches thus deployed temporal action as an "extension of their missionary functions,"[51] a unique situation in a broader context of Protestant hegemony in Afro-American religious organization. While Winston-Salem and Greenville are not similarly exceptional, Ladd's assessment of the prominence of ministerial leadership derives partly from a comparison with political leadership patterns outside the black community; in Winston-Salem only 22 percent of those identified as top black leaders were ministers and in Greenville only 28 percent, and in neither case was the black clergy in general involved in temporal affairs.[52] Despite the circumstance that—for several reasons—these rates are substantially higher than those prevailing among whites, the fact of the matter is that in Greenville more than 70 percent and in Winston-Salem more than 75 percent of black political leadership was based in secular occupations and institutions.

Yet the connection of the church with the development of politics in the black community is not a complete invention, even though claims concerning its leadership role are vastly exaggerated. A more accurate representation locates the church's role in protest politics mainly in provision of institutional support for activities initiated and led under other auspices. Chafe, for instance, notes that once civil rights activism took hold in Greensboro ministers gave vital assistance—under pressure from their activated congregations—by making church buildings and mimeograph facilities available to activists and "using their pulpits as vehicles for dispensing information about the boycott and protest activities."[53] This view is consistent with the earlier observations of Bunche, Davis, Frazier, Johnson, and Myrdal, who found the church's disposition toward political involvement to be governed by the existence of independent, secularly based initiatives to which clerical leadership was forced to respond. Their perceptions, moreover, were corroborated in the mid-1960s by Matthews and Prothro, whose study of a diverse sample of southern cities and counties indicated that the church became an arena for discussion of political issues only in direct relation to the existence and extent of black political organization outside the church. Where no extrinsic political organization existed, neither did the clergy engage political issues. They conclude: "When the Negro church gets into electoral politics . . . it is supplementing rather than substituting for more explicitly political organizations." [54]

Although the church's role in protest politics was a passive one, its function as a primary institution of community linkage constituted an important element in the contextual field within which mobilization strategies necessarily were elaborated. As the various case studies indicate, far from leading, the clergy all too frequently was *led* to support civil rights activity only through considerable pressure from popular community sentiment and specific demands from mobilized congregations. In this aspect, the church was less an agency of political action than another terrain for struggle by independently legitimated movement activists. Moreover, the object of that struggle may not have been so much the mantle of the clergy's moral authority as it was access to the material resources the church controlled as a temporal institution.

Even though its primacy in this regard receded with the development of black newspapers and the articulation of other institutions, the church generally remained an important mechanism of communication in the Afro-American community. Even in Durham respondents listed the church as most effective among a variety of communicative linkages between leaders and constituents. [55] Burgess identified the churches there as "the most comprehensive communication avenue available in the [black] sub-community," noting that they "serve as centers of organized social activity." [56] In other, less well differentiated communities the church's communicative functions were still more significant. Ladd, noting the contrast with nearby Durham and Raleigh, found the church paramount for dissemination of information in black Winston-Salem, Greenville, and similar locales. He also emphasized, like Chafe, the importance of church buildings as meeting sites for activist political groups.[57]

The church was a significant nexus for the movement in another sense that is distinct but not wholly separate from the communication function. McAdam observed that the church constituted, as did the schools and NAACP chapters, an "interactional [network] facilitating the 'bloc recruitment' of movement participants."[58] These networks were strategically important in that they enabled activist leadership "to recruit en masse along existing lines of interaction, thereby sparing themselves the much more difficult task of developing a membership from scratch."[59] In a reversal of Christ's injunction to his apostles, political activists went to the churches as "fishers of men" and women for unambiguously secular objectives. In the process, activists often succeeded in redefining the church's mission, at least temporarily. In church-based initiatives, for example, "it was not so much that movement participants were recruited from among the ranks of active churchgoers as it was a case of church membership itself being redefined to include movement participation as a primary requisite of the role."[60] This finding affirms Myrdal's contention that the black church simply expresses dispositions otherwise extant in the black community. Noting the rising protest in the 1940s, he averred that when "the Negro community changes, the church will also change" and predicted that increased political activism would bring demands on the church to engage itself in "the work for protest and betterment."[61]

While assertions of the church's centrality as a political institution among Afro-Americans are clearly questionable historically, demonstration to that effect does not exhaust the range of very problematic issues raised by the postulated linkage of church and politics. The faulty historical interpretation is a premise undergirding a relation posited in and for the present, and the two are separable inasmuch as the latter is advanced as an exhortation to action as well as an allegation of fact. Contemporary proclamation of the church's role in black politics carries a strategic imperative whose justification may be weakened by exposure of the falsity of its historical premises, but such disconfirmation does not completely undermine the proposition's hortatory component. Even a conclusive argument against the notion of a legacy of church-based politics leaves open questions concerning the efficacy and desirability of that kind of model in the here-and-now. These questions center theoretically on the appropriateness of the principles of representation and political authority which the church embodies in the black community.

Regarding the issue of representation, two fundamental problems confront assertions of an authenticating or primal leadership role for the church in Afro-American politics. In the first place, as I have argued earlier, the perception of the church as the ultimate source of authentic black political activity assumes as a precondition a pandemic black religiosity and church membership. However, while the church may be a more important institutional foundation of community life among Afro-Americans than among other groups, church affiliation hardly has been a universal characteristic of black American existence. Gosnell, in noting the significance of the churches as mobilization linkages in the 1930s, found that 50 percent of black voters in Chicago belonged to some church and that 25 percent attended Sunday services regularly.[62] Those rates of participation would make the church an attractive vehicle for political organization, but if it were thus to be seen as a mechanism for authenticating racial leadership, then what of the other half of the electorate, who—for whatever reasons—opted not to join a church? How are they represented? That question looms still greater in the contemporary period in which the church competes with a myriad of other bases of affiliation and identification in black communities, many of them electoral or otherwise directly political. To the extent that church-based networks are construed as sources for establishing authenticity of political spokesmanship, that segment of the race which chooses not to define itself through church or religious affiliation is in effect denied membership in the polity. Decline in black church membership since the 1930s only strengthens this observation.[63]

Reliance on church networks for validating claims to black leadership is strategically problematic in another sense as well. With regard to issues bearing on representation, the church is a politically redundant entity. Here it is important to distinguish acknowledgment of religious institutions' tactical support of political mobilization from the broader assertion of the church's centrality in black politics. The latter position interposes clerical authority between political spokesmanship aspirants and the racial constituency—in principle, a position that is incommensurate in a liberal, bourgeois society. However, in the context of systematic black exclusion from procedural channels of political participation, assignment of a surrogate role to the church might have been defensible on grounds of its relative institutional primacy and the elimination of more suitable alternatives. Even though the church typically did not exercise such political functions, exhortations that it should do so would be plausible and instrumentally reasonable in the absence of avenues for direct, systemic participation. However, with the removal of barriers blocking electoral participation, the notion of clerical or church-based political legitimation constitutes an unnecessary and dubious incursion into regular processes.

Strategic intervention by religious institutions into those processes is justifiable insofar as the church operates as one among an array of interest groups in the black community, pressing its specific agendas as such and not striving to enforce them as nonnegotiable collective racial interest. To that extent the politically engaged church subordinates itself to secular procedures. Assertions that organic, clerical legitimations preempt those procedures, on the contrary, remove churchly agendas from the arena of orderly public scrutiny and debate. The principle of religious superordination might adequately reflect the preferences of those who identify with the church, but it potentially sabotages democratic organization of the contemporary black polity. This is hardly to deny the possible limitations of electoral proceduralism; however, if commitment to the value of democracy is to be maintained, challenges to the adequacy of proceduralism must emanate from a more open and more extensively participatory standard of representation. Appeal to such a standard is conspicuously absent from notions alleging representative priority of church-based legitimations among Afro-Americans.

The rhetoric of organic or primalistic authenticity surrounding assertions of the church's special political status covers a model of authority that is antithetical to participatory representation. As Frazier indicated, "the pattern of control and organization of the Negro church has been authoritarian, with a strong man in a dominant position."[64] The basis of clerical authority lies outside the temporal world and is not susceptible to secular dispute. The community constituted in the church is not reproduced through open discourse but is bound by consensual acceptance of a relation that vests collective judgment in the charismatic authority of the minister. The status of superordinate ministerial authority can be acquired through vocation or being "called." However, once attained, that status uncouples the minister from the body of the faithful and—because of the assumption of privileged clerical access to divine purposes mysterious to others—exonerates clerical leadership from susceptibility to secular criticism.

This model of authority is fundamentally antiparticipatory

and antidemocratic; in fact, it is grounded on a denial of the rationality that democratic participation requires. Diane Johnson, in an essay that includes the distinctive style of black charismatic religion among several factors that led to the massacre at Jonestown, observes that this black religious style devalues ''the powers of analysis and penetration that education supposedly confers.'' Black ministers, she notes, ''in particular sustain a traditional style of histrionic worship in which real and false prophets are . . . easily confused.''[65] Frazier argues, moreover, that because of its important role in the social organization of the black community, the church's distinctive patterns of authority have exerted a powerful authoritarian force in the elaboration of Afro-American institutions in general, a consequence of which has been a chronic and extensive undervaluation of democratic processes in the black community. The church and religion, Frazier concludes, ''have cast a shadow over the entire intellectual life of Negroes.''[66] This antiparticipatory and antiintellectual impetus deauthorizes the principle of individual autonomy, which is the basis of citizenship, and—when combined with the church's intrinsically antitemporal eschatological orientation—mandates quietism, political and otherwise.

Gary Marx's study of the relationship of religious and political attitudes in the black community discloses the church's empirical impact on black political culture. Marx found an inverse relation prevailing between intensity of religious belief and practice and intensity of support for political activism among a national metropolitan sample of black attitudes at the height of the civil rights movement. Specifically, disposition toward militance in support of civil rights agendas increased steadily with decreasing subjective importance assigned to religion.[67] The more orthodox were respondents' religious beliefs, the less likely were they to be politically militant.[68] The more frequently respondents attended church, the weaker was their support for activism.[69] When responses were combined into a cumulative index of religiosity, the results were most striking. The inverse relation persisted, and the variance was definitive. Only 26 percent of those scoring "very religious" favored political militancy, but 70 percent of the "not at all religious" were so inclined.[70] Moreover, the basic inverse relation held across all levels of education, age groups, regions, both sexes, and all denominational affiliations.[71] Among denominations, Methodists and Baptists—by far the largest groupings in the black population—scored lowest on the militancy scale; a residual category, "Sects and cults"—including Pentecostals, Jehovah's Witnesses, and other flotsam and jetsam of the religious universe—scored lowest of all.[72] This finding challenges the arguments of those such as Cornel West who identify the "evangelical and pietistic" tendency in black religion as the source of emancipatory theory and politics in the black community.[73] Regarding the Baptists—the largest single black denomination—J. H. Jackson, longtime president of the National Baptist Convention, not only endorsed Reagan in 1980 but resisted the surge of black political activism throughout the civil rights movement and beyond.[74]

Marx's findings are made all the more salient by the fact that his research was conducted in 1964, during the most active phase of black protest politics. The church's claim to preemptive political authenticity rests largely on evocative images of clerical or church-based activation of popular resistance during that period. Jesse Jackson, as we have seen, from beginning to end deployed that imagery—along with the general principle of clerical authority—to legitimize his candidacy. However, not only does examination reveal the church at most to have been *led* from a characteristic stance of accommodating and rationalizing the status quo of racial subordination to association with a movement that was a fait accompli, but, even when activism was greatest in the black community, church identification clearly remained an alternative to political action. Nevertheless, the mythology of

church-based politics lingers, and the Jackson initiative seems
to have rekindled its fires. Still, given the models of authority
and participation for which the church stands, its projection
as a major black political force insinuates between black citizens and their political representation a mediation that is justifiable neither in relation to need or utility nor in the name
of a larger vision of social emancipation.[75]

The fundamental tension between the church and politics
in the black community—both historically and in the present—resonates with the critique of religion developed by Karl
Marx in the 1840s:

> This state, this society, produce religion, an inverted
> *world-consciousness,* because they are an *inverted world.*
> Religion is the general theory of that world . . . its logic
> in a popular form, its spiritualistic *point d'honneur,* its
> enthusiasm, its moral sanction, its solemn complement,
> its universal source of consolation and justification. . . .
> *Religious* distress is at the same time the *expression* of
> real distress and also the *protest* against real distress. Re-
> ligion is the sign of the oppressed creature, the heart of a
> heartless world, just as it is the spirit of spiritless condi-
> tions. It is the *opium* of the people. . . . Religion is only
> the illusory sun which revolves around man as long as he
> does not revolve round himself.[76]

The domain of the black church has been the spiritual and
institutional adaptation of Afro-Americans to an apparently
inexorable context of subordination and dispossession. It has
been at various points in this century a central conduit for the
reproduction of community life under severely restricted conditions. Whether the church's acquiescence to the unpalatable
secular order has been equally central in legitimizing those
conditions or whether another course was even possible are
issues open to debate. However, it is clear that the church's
functionality as an integrative institution, as well as its vaunted

success as a source of hope in a temporal situation apparently hopeless, has been predicated on acceptance of the essential structure of the world of material social and political relations as given. To that extent, the black church has developed as an inherently noninterventionist, and thus conservative quasi-secular institution.

The realm of politics by definition is temporal intervention. Its object is action within and therefore practical "criticism of the *vale* of *tears,* the *halo* of which is religion."[77] The ambivalent historical role of the church in Afro-American politics is in this sense an expression not only of practical organizational tensions but of an essential incompatibility, if not antagonism, of institutional logics and functions. The problem at the core of the political mythology of the black church is not simply its historical inaccuracy or even its disturbing implications for the development and maintenance of rational, democratic discourse in the black community. A matter for equal concern is that the projection of the church as the source of leadership authenticity assigns responsibility for political legitimation to an intrinsically antipolitical agency.

i.e. The moral majority?

5

The Crisis of Political Agenda in the Black Community

The propagation of the mythology of the political black church has been abetted by the reluctance of the secular elites to challenge it. No doubt many of those elites genuinely adhere to the mythology themselves, but another source of this reluctance may lie in the mythology's relation to actual or potential problems currently surrounding elite legitimacy in the black community. As I have argued in chapter 1, black political leadership of both electoral and protest types finds itself steadily less capable of generating programmatic responses adequate to the needs of their generalized black constituencies. At least three factors account for their declining effectiveness, and each potentially undermines legitimacy.

61

Sources of the Crisis of Political Direction

First, black elites' capacity to deliver payoffs has been a function of the combined effect of extrasystemic pressure and participation in the broader governing consensus regnant in American politics since the Second World War, anchored in the Democratic party. In this sense a major outcome of 1960s activism was the formalization of a status for blacks within the political coalition that advocated the stimulation of economic growth as the basis for social cohesion.

As black voters joined the key sectors of Democratic electoral support (along with labor unions, Catholics, Jews, and southern whites), black elites also joined the calculus of allocation of the proceeds of economic and social growth—the pluralist porkbarrel.[1] The increasing significance of the black vote for Democratic purposes outside the South led the party to at least tepid support of civil rights protest activity, which in turn was integrated into the growth consensus through programmatic articulation of a civil rights agenda that simply factored blacks into the distributive queue. This coalition began to unravel with the decline of growth in the 1970s.[2] Yet current black political leadership has structured its definitions of racial needs and strategies entirely around assumptions of protected status in the foundering coalition. To that extent, those elites have little critical leverage from which to apprehend and adjust to the changing social management environment. As a consequence their capacity to deliver collective payoffs is diminished.

A second and related factor is the particularly obdurate posture adopted toward black-identified allocations by the Reagan regime's "program for recovery," its practical proposal for the basis of a new, recomposed growth coalition. The steady flow of statistics demonstrating the detrimental impact of Reagan administration policies on blacks reminds one of the Vietnam-era body counts that quickly became a desensitizing barrage. Nevertheless, two recent findings are illustrative. Between January 1981 and the summer of 1984 white longterm unemployment increased 1.5 percent; among blacks, however, the rate of increase was 72 percent.[3] Moreover, Bawden and Palmer found that if all budget reductions proposed by the Reagan administration had been enacted, the following programs with disproportionately black constituencies would have been cut by the following amounts: Legal Services, 100 percent; Public Service Employment, 100 percent; Aid to Families with Dependent Children, 28 percent; Employment and Training, 43.9 percent; Compensatory Education, 61 percent; Financial Aid for Needy Students, 68.9 percent; Work Incentive Program, 100 percent; Food Stamps, 51.7 percent; and Child Nutrition, 46 percent.[4] Along with the administration's official and symbolic association with other overtures that augur the dismantling of federal commitment to civil rights enforcement, these findings transmit an unambiguous message that entrenched black elites have little clout in Reagan's proposed consensus. Not only do blacks suffer the brunt of Reagan's program for reconstituting a growth agenda, but the administration's intransigence punctuates the essential powerlessness of black leadership.

The third condition limiting black leadership's political capacity, ironically, is a function of successful entrenchment. Integration of black elites into the growth calculus, as I have argued, has opened opportunities for upwardly mobile blacks—thereby segmenting the black population economically into a relatively secure stratum at one end and a dispossessed, optionless component at the other. A report for the Joint Center for Political Studies reveals that, whereas in the 1960-70 period the proportions of black low income families decreased and high income families increased at roughly the same impressive rate, between 1970 and 1979 the shares of families in both categories increased. In 1970, 30.6 percent of black families earned in the low income range and 35.2 percent in the high income. In 1979 32.5 percent were low income and 38.6 percent high income, while the middle income component fell from 34.2 percent in 1970 to 28.9 percent in 1979. Between 1979 and 1982 the low income category rose steadily to 37.8 percent; the high income category dropped to just over 35 percent in 1981 and stabilized at that level, while middle income families continued to decline, reaching 26.9 percent in 1982.[5] Distribution of wealth by asset category, perhaps a more telling measure of economic mobility, is equally instructive. While the proportions of total black wealth represented by equity in homes (the largest single category) and vehicles and in financial assets declined slightly between 1967 and 1979, equity in rental or other property more than doubled, from 12 percent to 25 percent of the total.[6] Definition of a disproportionately elite-serving agenda—focused on elaboration of compensatory measures to extend equality of opportunity to the upwardly mobile—has fueled economic polarization in the black community.[7]

The integration of black elites into the old growth coalition has distanced them from their rank-and-file black constituencies in three distinct spheres. Politically, integration provides a formal alternative to constituent linkages as a source of elite legitimation; articulation of claims through the coalition's protocorporatist negotiation processes seems, relative to popular issue generation, a more orderly, commodious, and pragmatically rational procedure for defining and pressing racial agendas. Sociologically, integration enmeshes black leadership structurally within an external reference group, a broader community of elite-pluralistic discourse and meaning organized around social management by means of nonredistributive allocations to designated status groups.[8] The combined weight of those two dynamics enhances natural tendencies toward economic differentiation in the black community as elites have consolidated their privileged status programmatically. Thus, the focus of the racial agenda articulated by black leadership has shifted increasingly over the 1970s and

1980s to: (a) affirmative action, which benefits the upwardly mobile disproportionately—though not exclusively; (b) high-status job appointments; and (c) specification of set-asides for minority contractors.[9]

It may well be that the sanction against redistribution—especially in a context of receding growth—has so circumscribed the field of options that a more comprehensive racial program is impracticable. If so, concentration on a relatively limited elite-serving agenda might arguably be a reasonable optimizing strategy.

Focusing at the admittedly more narrow local level, Paul Peterson demonstrates how the pluralist decisional processes operative in growth politics convert potentially redistributive demands into "manageable" agenda items. He notes that when "groups demand redistributive reforms . . . government leaders explore ways of disaggregating the proposals so that from the resources available to them they can make some response."[10] A variant of this strategy entails "identification of group leaders and giving them special concessions . . . [they] can be employed in relevant public-service positions, given an honored position in policy deliberations, or invited to participate in conferences at distant places." Peterson acknowledges the sociologically integrative dynamic at work in these processes in observing that by "being exposed to the problems of formulating adequate responses to redistributive demands, these leaders, without necessarily giving up their objectives, are encouraged to channel their energies into more realistic approaches."[11] Determination of the magnitude of "resources available" is, despite Peterson's emphasis on objective limits, in large measure a political decision, derived from the configurations of interest considered significant and the intensity of commitment to a given pattern of allocation. However, once such a determination is made, it is enforceable on all claimant groups that seek to participate in the growth-driven system.

Although national policy processes are more open to redistributive claims, the same logic operates at that level, and its tracings become more visible as the promise of unlimited growth wanes. In this environment an objective of cutting losses by safeguarding elite gains, while hardly altruistic, may be the only systemically consistent adaptation to retrenchment. In any event, an alternative course might require disruption of systemic governing processes, a project which jeopardizes the basis of elite status.[12]

No matter whether other acceptable options exist, black political leadership currently rests precariously at the nexus of these three corrosive forces: (1) the collapse of the Democratic growth coalition in which the systemic linkages of Afro-American politics are embedded; (2) the aggressively anti-black stance of Reaganism; and (3) the widening economic gap separating components of the black community. In this circumstance political elites predictably exhibit signs of failure of nerve and give vent to considerable soul-searching.[13] Their capacity to deliver collective goods from the porkbarrel has been destabilized, and—as they have been forced to bear the message of diminishing expectations to a constituency already suffering economic marginalization—they become ever more attentive to problems of legitimation. Inability to respond effectively to deteriorating conditions raises the possibility of constituent disaffection, and elite cautiousness is no doubt compounded by recurring querulousness in the media with regard to the efficacy of black political spokesmanship in general.[14]

At this point the successful incorporation of black leadership into regular channels of policy negotiation becomes a mixed blessing; inasmuch as functioning in those channels requires internalization of the nonredistributive rules of the game, the inability to advance the concrete interests of a substantial element of the black constituency is the price of "effective" participation. This situation portends that entrenched political elites' legitimacy may be vulnerable to challenges from below in the black community. Concern in this regard is no doubt heightened by the spokesmanship stratum's customary inclination to mobilize black support with a campaign rhetoric that both harkens images of protest activism and exaggerates the outcomes attainable through systemic action; chickens, one might say, threaten to come home to roost.

The Jackson Campaign and the Crisis

The fragile, ambivalent position of black political elites was adumbrated through the 1984 Jackson phenomenon, as well as the churchly mythology attendant to it. It is safe to assume that the less than enthusiastic reaction to Jackson's proposed candidacy by official black elites on its face mainly reflected territorial defensiveness.

Criticisms proferred by Coleman Young and others bluntly castigated the aspiring candidate for attempting to catapult himself over the domain of elected officials. Yet, once Jackson began to propagate the image of his bypassing elite opposition by going directly to the masses, all except the most recalcitrant opponents matter-of-factly either succumbed to or were pacified by the campaign's lure. Hardbitten politicians, unlikely to be swayed by an initiative based on ephemera such as creating positive images and establishing collective "respect," became converts to Jackson's cause and adopted its vague precepts. Pragmatically astute political elites should not have been brought into line by the orchestrated show purported to demonstrate an early groundswell of popular support; nevertheless they accepted and repeated Jackson's claim with little reservation, thereby helping to make it real. Their crumbling before Jackson's proclamations reflects the extent of the crisis of purpose and direction in which they are mired.

On one level, the Jackson bandwagon effectively disclosed, more than suspension of disbelief, an active willingness to believe, scarcely appearing chastened by *realpolitik.*

Questions about the campaign's lack of a programmatic agenda, lack of clarity concerning its party objectives, or projection of options for the postprimary period either did not surface as strategic questions or were rebuffed as misanthropy. Instead, profusions of unbounded enthusiasm blustered past these and other issues pertinent to assessment of the propriety of a presidential campaign. Jackson's instrumental and expressive claims remained essentially confounded throughout the primary season, and his failure to distinguish them generated little criticism within his camp.

This willingness to suspend critical judgment may reflect—in addition to the "spirit of spiritless conditions," the blind optimism that accompanies the absence of palpable options—the entrenched political elites' hypersensitivity to the specter of popular black discontent. Because they have been able neither to fulfill the "promises of power" described by Carl Stokes—in the halcyon days of their systemic integration—[15] nor to exert a viable counterforce to later retrenchment against Afro-American aspirations, black political leadership might well have sensed that Jackson's contentions implying their alienation from the popular black constituency could reverberate beyond the issue of his candidacy. Subsequent indications—as in the case of Julian Bond's uncharacteristically close race against a marginal opponent—suggest that disaffection may be sufficiently extensive within the black community that it can be galvanized to overcome the typically heavy weight of incumbency.[16]

From this perspective, climbing onto the Jackson bandwagon might have been an instrumentally attractive course in two respects for black elites disconcerted by possible legitimacy deficits. By assisting in defining the basis of cleavage in the black community in terms of a transitory concern such as the status of Jackson's candidacy, support for the campaign may have functioned to direct latent black political discontent toward unsupportive spokespersons defined as race-traitors, thereby deflecting it from issues pertaining to the general efficacy of entrenched political elites. A corollary effect is that definition of support for Jackson as the elemental criterion of racial loyalty provided an easy test of legitimacy. Additionally, the cathartic nature of Jackson's appeal, along with the correlative ideological mystique of a church-based politics, provided a diffuse, yet well contained arena for the expression of black alienation—a semblance of mass political activation without the volatility of substantive intervention. That the expressive energies thus mobilized could dissipate into deeper estrangement and resignation is another matter. Further, that possibility may not be a source of much real concern; for not only do legitimation problems constitute a more immediate threat to elite status, but under the prevailing styles of black political spokesmanship popular participation is neither necessary nor especially desirable.

It might be tempting to argue that entrenched elites in some degree coopted the campaign to serve their own purposes. The critical flaw of such an argument, however, is that Jackson himself and his presidential initiative were situated within the black political elite structure from the first. As I have shown in chapter 2, Jackson's attentive public was drawn from upper income, upwardly mobile strata in the black community.[17] He undertook to broach the putative tension between mass and elite agendas only after failing to generate a consensus around support for his effort in internal elite circles. Indeed, Jackson has been the major proponent of the most elite-centered tendency in contemporary racial advocacy, the "corporate interventionist" orientation, which is profoundly antipopular in two senses. First, benefits sought and derived by this approach are concentrated among businessmen and other upper status blacks. Second, this strategy of racial brokerage, in uncoupling from state processes, is removed from arenas of public scrutiny and participation. It endorses instead a principle of decisionmaking via exclusively private negotiation between corporate and advocacy organization elites; the popular constituency figures into this engineering process only as the bargaining capital represented in the dubious threat of boycott, the objectified leverage of an extortionist bluff.[18]

The Structural Dynamics of the Jackson Campaign

Notwithstanding its pretensions to political revitalization, the Jackson initiative proposed no substantive departure from the morass in which black political elites are trapped. The campaign reproduced the larger crisis of purpose and direction in its inability to generate a coherent political program or discrete policy agenda. Jackson's ambivalent intentions no doubt contributed to the difficulty in fashioning a consistent set of public policy stances. His candidacy never selected a principal orientation between the options of practical contention for the nomination—an impossibility in any event—or representation of a particular critical vision. Despite the media coverage his effort garnered, it was not credible as an instrumental activity directed toward influencing the nomination because after the Illinois primary at the latest it obviously had no chance to win enough delegates to affect the outcome of the convention. At the same time, Jackson's initiative had little authenticity as a protest candidacy because it never clearly specified the nature of the protest.

Furthermore, the campaign did not reconcile the antinomical images with which it sought to associate itself. Jackson was proferred as the emblem of a transracial, transethnic coalition of the disaffected—the "Rainbow Coalition"—and as the embodiment of a uniquely black assertiveness, reflected in the slogan, "It's our time now." The objective of amassing votes, because the black community was Jackson's only base of electoral support, subordinated development of a public policy issue agenda to emotional, distinctively racial appeal. Yet the desire to assert a global ''moral force'' in American politics warranted cultivation of a wider constituency which could be created only through projection of national policy positions. The Jackson forces never clarified the relation of these contrary, although perhaps not intrinsically contradictory, appeals. The campaign resolved this problem practically by settling into a fundamentally racial strategy onto which overtures toward a broader public were affixed desultorily.[19] The outcome was a perfunctory set of platform demands that scarcely represented the concerns of Jackson's almost totally black electoral constituency and which, therefore, the dominant Mondale forces at the convention could reject with ease.

Its ambivalence, though, is not the ultimate cause of the campaign's failure to develop a political program. Indeed, the vacillation implies an already existent programmatic insolvency. Definitive choices of focus and constituency were avoided in the last analysis because the Jackson forces had no firm, purposeful basis upon which to make them. Jackson's candidacy was not constrained by the disciplining strategic imperatives that would impel a campaign geared toward concrete objectives—for instance, building steadily toward electoral majority or some other empirically realizable end informing tactical activity. The campaign also lacked any overriding ideological vision that might have provided an alternative framework which could integrate and discipline tactics and possibly stimulate organizational coherence. The absence of goals—mundane or transcendent—that were explicit and specified instrumentally left a conceptual void which, given the campaign's pressing need to gather votes, was filled by adoption of utility in relation to the shifting requirements of image projection as a core strategic principle.

The campaign's want of a structure of meaning deeper than superficial candidate packaging is more the source of the effort's ambivalence than its consequence. The converse argument would be more plausible if Jackson's candidacy could be shown to have vacillated between alternative policy agendas. Rather, alternation of essentially imagistic appeals to coexistent, parallel constituencies substituted for development of a political program. In addition to the vicissitudes of Jackson's mercurial personal style, moreover, this circumstance also reproduces a distinctive attribute of contemporary black political leadership behavior.

In 1972, during his first successful campaign for Georgia's fifth congressional district seat, Andrew Young—later Carter's United Nations ambassador and then elected mayor of Atlanta in 1981—consented to make a presentation to a political science departmental seminar at the predominantly black Atlanta University. Faculty and graduate students had come with expectations that Young would discuss his program, clarifying media reports of controversial positions that he had enunciated before white audiences—opposition to abortion, advocacy of saturation bombing in what was then North Vietnam, and so on. Instead, Young expatiated for three quarters of an hour on the need to turn out the vote for his election and on the irresponsibility that black voters had exhibited in that regard in his 1970 defeat. Finally, a bemused graduate student, a Young supporter, politely observed that the candidate had not addressed any matters of local or national policy and inquired as to the specific components of his issue agenda. Young replied that he had been so preoccupied with running for office that he simply had not had time to develop policy positions. However, he assured, once elected he would as a first priority study "the issues" and formulate positions on them. Besides, he noted, policy positions were of little moment because blacks had no option other than to vote for him anyway, since his opponent was a white Republican. Twelve years later Jesse Jackson contested for the Democratic presidential nomination on a similar basis.

This outlook, to be sure, reflects the cathartic and authoritarian dynamics at work in Afro-American politics. But it also indicates the extent to which present black political elites are bound by the conceptual and programmatic strictures of the model of growth politics within which their status is constituted. That model has been the matrix for the development of their careers and political capacity for at least two decades. Its internalized logic and structures have formed the phenomenal field for black spokespersons, their incognizant life-world. Questions of national direction were irrelevant to Andrew Young in 1972 because acceptance of a pregiven national growth agenda was an elemental condition of black systemic political integration.[20] The heteronomous and antidiscursive characteristics of black political culture only deepened the opacity of this relation and its presuppositions. Because the development of post–civil rights era black elites has been inextricably connected with and dependent on the Democratic growth coalition, its breakdown leaves them without a point of reference, with neither a perspective on its decomposition nor a language of response. Jesse Jackson may be limited in his capacity for programmatic vision by his idiosyncratic opportunism, inconstancy, and self-aggrandizement. However, as the enthusiasm of his elite support demonstrates, his lack of critical direction resonates with a much more general state of affairs in the black community. Nothing reveals the magnitude of this paralysis more vividly than the emptiness of Jackson's platform demands to the Democratic convention.

Jackson's Convention Strategy— Plus ça Change. . . .

In April 1984 two political scientists associated with the Jackson campaign proposed an outline for a rudimentary "liberal-progressive agenda for any candidate who would seek to represent the Black community in presidential politics."[21] The minimal components of their laundry list of concerns were:

(1) national economic reconstruction aimed toward full employment; (2) welfare reform targeting the unemployed and underemployed as well as other dependent groups; (3) comprehensive national health insurance; (4) educational reform with particular focus on securing access to child care and higher education; (5) reorientation of military budgets and defense priorities; (6) national industrial policy; and (7) more affirmative action.[22] By contrast, the bill of particulars presented to the Democratic platform committee by Jesse Jackson, the authors' candidate of choice, consisted of the following items: (1) a pledge that the United States and its NATO allies would never authorize a nuclear first strike; (2) four-year reductions in military spending; (3) commitment to affirmative action; and (4) elimination of runoff primaries.[23] At most, the Jackson agenda addressed only two of the seven items that Smith and McCormick held to comprise the barest skeleton of black priorities. Although it is quite probable that Afro-Americans generally would support a no-first-strike commitment and that blacks have as much stake in that issue as any other group in the polity, that proposed platform amendment cannot be considered a distinctively black concern. Nor was the runoff primary—which Jackson touted as a critical "litmus test" of "respect" for black interests—generally perceived as a vital issue in the black community.

In fact, the runoff primary issue is an emblem of the campaign's programmatic capriciousness. The runoff primary is a practice followed in some form in not more than ten states, nine of which are in the South. This practice requires that in party primaries in which no candidate receives a clear majority of votes cast, the two contenders with the greatest vote totals meet in a second election to determine the nominee. This provision, which dates from the first decades of this century, subsequently has carried the stigma of association with other measures adopted to disfranchise Afro-Americans.[24] Whether functional disfranchisement has been an actual intention or an unintended byproduct of the dual primary system is a matter of some controversy. However, it is clear that in many jurisdictions, given strong patterns of racial bloc voting, the practice hinders—if not flatly prevents—black candidates from winning party nomination primaries.[25]

In districts in which blacks comprise less than a majority of the electorate, black candidates might benefit from fragmentation of white votes by gaining pluralities in primary elections. Institution of a runoff primary, however, removes this potential advantage by requiring an absolute electoral majority as the criterion of victory. Elimination of runoff primaries thus could assist black candidates' electoral chances where the following conditions obtain: "(1) racial bloc voting; (2) blacks are in a minority; (3) whites split their votes between 2 or more candidates; (4) blacks vote unanimously for a black candidate."[26] There are approximately thirteen southern congressional seats held by whites whose districts are in runoff primary states and are 30–49 percent black;[27] Jackson and other opponents of the second primary presume that its abolition would improve the likelihood of black electoral success in those and similarly composed jurisdictions. So it was that the runoff primary—despite nearly universal indifference expressed by black voters[28]—became the campaign's pivotal "black" issue at the Democratic convention.

The presumption underlying this focus is simplistic on two counts. In the first place concentration on the dual primary procedure ironically overlooks the more fundamental dynamic, that is, the dominant pattern of racial bloc voting. As Steve Suitts, executive director of the Southern Regional Council, noted in his testimony before John Conyers's House Judiciary Subcommittee on Civil and Constitutional Rights, removal of second primaries may increase the number of black candidates winning Democratic nominations in black minority jurisdictions at the price of enhancing Republican success in general elections.[29] H. M. Michaux, a Jackson confidant, acknowledged that the proposed reform could be expected to strengthen the Republican party's momentum in the South.[30] Michaux, who lost a runoff for a North Carolina congressional seat in 1982 and suggested opposition to dual primaries as a Jackson campaign item, was unperturbed by that consequence, implying that accelerating realignment could purify the Democrats as a minority party. Jackson, however, contended that defeat of Reaganism ranked highest among his immediate objectives,[31] and to that extent his adoption of the runoff primary issue as a demand on principle seems at least insufficiently thoughtful. The problem is that improving the prospects of black officeseekers does not exhaust the category of black electoral interests. Given patterns of racial voting, many situations exist—especially in the South—in which blacks cannot hope to elect black candidates; in those districts electoral interests probably are best pursued through coalescence with groups outside the black community. In a context in which the Republican program is wedded at all levels to an elementally antiblack agenda, the Democratic party offers the only real, though hardly ideal, arena for coalitional activity. Concentration on the runoff primary does not account for either the demographic and ideological constraints that limit black office seeking in those jurisdictions or the possibilities for other modes of electoral engagement. This focus is not only shallow analytically; it expresses a quite troubling disposition to reduce the objective of black political activity to one of its instruments, that is, election of black officials.

The second difficulty with the runoff primary is that despite its traditional association with black exclusion, in the current situation in the South it works both ways. In jurisdictions that are 50–60 percent black, second primaries can protect black candidates just as easily as they can frustrate electoral ambitions in other contexts. In Atlanta's 1981 mayoral race, for example, two ostensibly strong black contenders ran against a consensus white candidate. Andrew Young won a very slim plurality in the first primary and then defeated his white challenger handily in the runoff. If the other black contender had run nearly so well as had been forecast (as it turned out, he failed to carry a single precinct), Young would have finished second, and in the absence of a second primary he would have lost.

Despite the high visibility and strategic enticement of the 30–49 percent black congressional districts, the watershed of black electoral success comes with attainment of majority status in a jurisdiction.[32] The very strong tendency to racially determined voting suggests not only that black plurality Democratic victories would be cancelled by white defection to Republican opponents but also that abolition of dual primaries could increase the vulnerability of black candidates in jurisdictions with slim black majorities, a category which includes a growing proportion of all black elected officials.[33] Revealingly, Hosea Williams, who as an activist in Jackson's campaign vociferously denounced the dual primary, dropped his opposition to runoff elections when he contested against a white incumbent for a seat from Georgia's 60 percent black fifth congressional district. Williams admitted bluntly that elimination of the runoff would adversely affect his chances since the race featured more than one black candidate.[34] The point is that the dual primary is a very complex issue, and, short of a comprehensive, regionwide survey of electoral jurisdictions, it is impossible to assess the system's overall impact in the contemporary setting. The Jackson forces' apparent inclination to stake the race's political fortunes on so ambiguous an issue may have derived in part from naivete—notwithstanding the prominence of political scientists in the campaign's inner circles—or desperation born of lack of a clear purpose. From another perspective, however, the campaign's simplistic assault on the runoff primary may have indicated just the opposite of intentional naivete—subordination of a policy agenda to immediate self-promotion.

Shortly before the convention Ronald Walters argued for acceptance of Jackson's platform and other demands on an instrumental basis that had little manifest connection with influencing public policy. Adducing a need to make Jackson supporters feel that their votes had counted for something, Walters insisted that the demands should be met as an acknowledgment of the campaign's entitlement to party spoils. He contended that it was "not a question of giving us something that we have not won. It is a question of having played fairly."[35] Similarly, Jackson based his defense of the various demands—ranging from consideration as a vice-presidential nominee through party rule changes and platform issues to Mondale/Ferraro campaign staff appointments—on a requirement to recognize his alleged status as a powerful figure. The candidate asserted that he should have been included among Mondale's list of prospective runningmates because he had earned "peer group status" in the party.[36] Asked in early July to specify the campaign's terms for accommodation to an eventual Mondale-led ticket, Arnold Pinkney (then Jackson's campaign director) replied, "Rev. Jackson has to be given respect. He's earned it; entitled to it."[37] Jackson's postconvention demand for an expanded black presence in the Mondale campaign apparatus reduced quickly to a more specific demand for appointment of Jackson-supporting blacks to campaign positions; this specification naturally produced conflicts with those blacks who had been in Mondale's camp all along and who felt, not unreasonably, that they had prior claims on the campaign.[38]

6

Elite Self-Interest and Tension with Labor

The rhetoric of "respect" which Jackson mobilized as the justification for his various demands reduced the components of his issue agenda to the solipsistic objective of consolidating his personal status as a force in the Democratic party. The Jackson camp defined the significance of its demands less in terms of their intrinsic legitimacy than as expressions of Jackson's general capacity to wrench concessions. To that extent the purported merits of his agenda were of secondary importance at best. Overriding weight was attached to validating Jackson's brokerage status.[1]

In that context the jerry-built character of the platform proposals becomes understandable, as does the fact that Jackson concocted a new "litmus test," the demand that Mondale endorse a public employment jobs bill, only well after the platform debates and the convention had ended.[2] The two-month charade in which the erstwhile candidate constantly alternated statements of conciliation and support for Mondale with threats to withhold "enthusiasm" and attempts to extract an escalating, apparently arbitrary list of concessions undermines the contention that his initiative was grounded in any coherent social vision.[3] As columnist James Reston—in commenting on Jackson's continuing projection of new conditions to assure his involvement on behalf of the Mondale ticket—noted astutely, "There is no evidence in all his torrents of chautauqual rhetoric of any coherent plan. . . . Most of his policies could be expressed on a bumper sticker."[4]

Although the Jackson initiative's programmatic shallowness was clearly visible, Reston's criticism was an isolated acknowledgment to that effect. And black political leadership was conspicuously silent on that score, especially during the months between the Democratic convention and the presidential election. Indeed, such opposition as Jackson had met from black elites never focused on issues of political program anyway. However, once his initiative became a springboard from which to assert leverage in party circles, his vacuous language that reduced political interest to questions of collective "pride," "respect," and "enthusiasm" came to suffuse Afro-American elite political discourse, and his star became an attractive hitchingpost for a broad array of spokespersons.

Black columnists and commentators reproduced Jackson's essential definition of the appropriate modes and objectives of political activity without reservation. Roger Wilkins, who less than three years earlier had rejected hopes for emergence of a single black leader as categorically inappropriate, proclaimed that Jackson "is going to be there at the heart of things, arranging and rearranging in such fundamental ways that long after he is gone, it will be hard to remember what politics in the United States was like before he was around."[5] James Turner, director of Cornell's Africana Studies and Research Center, charged the Democrats with "not respecting [Jackson's] voice, and symbolically we were trying to speak through him.'' ''White people,'' Turner observed, ''seem incapable of giving us respect.''[6] Wilkins joined him both in subsuming black aspirations into Jackson's effort to enhance his status in the Democratic hierarchy and in doing so through the Jackson-authorized discursive code grounded on ''enthusiasm'' and ''respect'' as primally significant criteria governing political activity. The key to this code, of course, is that respect for Jackson yields enthusiasm among the black population as a whole.[7] Chet Fuller of the *Atlanta Constitution* asserted that Jackson had won ''abstract and symbolic victories''—however those might be measured—that were not only ''impressive'' but moreover ''had left an indelible mark on the American political process.''[8] Jay T. Harris, ''minority correspondent'' for the Gannett News Service, editorialized a fear that Mondale's ''failure to quickly appoint well-known and respected black politicians to senior posts in his campaign organization'' had dampened ''excitement and enthusiasm'' among the black electorate.[9] Ronald Smothers effused that Jackson's Rainbow candidacy had fueled a new ''enthusiasm'' among minority voters which was the basis of increases in registration.[10]

At the same time, the ''black leadership family'' readily embraced the insistence on publicly visible demonstrations of ''respect'' that the Jackson phenomenon spawned. In late August a group including nationally prominent elected officials and representatives of major racial advocacy organizations met with Mondale in Minnesota to negotiate an agenda that would ensure black support for the Mondale/Ferraro ticket. The group presented the following ''concerns'' in an advance mailgram sent over the signature of Richard Hatcher, Mayor of Gary and Jackson's campaign chairman:

(1) Black input on the expenditure of the $30 billion for social programs; (2) A major domestic policy speech on or about Aug. 29 which includes black issues ([Rep.

Charles] Rangel and [Rep. Walter] Fauntroy involved);
(3) Senior black policy person—public announcement;
(4) One-half of voter registration funds under control of
[Jackson adviser and Mondale staff appointee] Ernie
Greene for black voter registration programs throughout
the nation; (5) Meeting with blacks at invitation of Vice
President Mondale (Mondale must attend), Gerry [Fer-
raro] and all senior staff within next 10 days per Ernie
Greene; (6) Major foreign policy address that covers all
black international concerns; C. Rangel and W. Fauntroy
for input; (7) on-going regular base touching with Beckel
by Hatcher group.[11]

In uniting to formulate and press that agenda the group
demonstrated their abilities to capitalize on the situation created by Jackson's definition of the driving forces of black
politics. That they did so was testimony to this national leadership cohort's astuteness as pragmatic political actors. However, the agenda itself—which Jackson helped to develop and
endorsed—betrayed the deeper impasse in which they were
mired. The group's demands of Mondale attained specificity
only as they expressed the desire for formal involvement; the
ends for which consultative status was sought were not explicitly articulated, except as they concerned black representation in the dispensation of campaign spoils. The demand for
"input" on social program expenditures was not accompanied by recommendations for program priorities. Nor did the
Hatcher group make any allusion to the specific content of
the domestic "black issues" and "black international concerns" which it insisted that Mondale address; the only concrete proposals contained in those demands concerned designation of Rangel and Fauntroy—the former a Mondale
supporter and the latter a member of the Jackson camp—as
representatives of an official black presence.
The problem disclosed by the focus of the Hatcher group's

agenda is not simple opportunism. On the contrary, lobbying to enhance status in the party governing apparatus is a standard, and certainly appropriate, practice among participating elites. To that extent the group's posture affirms the successful integration of black elites into systemic processes. Without detracting from this demonstration of systemic political capacity, however, the group's overture underscores the Afro-American elite's general failure of political vision. This failure is particularly striking in light of the current disarray within the Democratic coalition and the debate over the character of its reconstitution. Unlike the AFL-CIO, for example, which opted for a coherent policy agenda to combat the rightist mood,[12] black leadership clung to a business-as-usual orientation circumscribed by the logic of securing leverage as a status group.

This reaction is a reasonable response to concern that an apparent right-wing groundswell in the society potentially relegates Afro-Americans to the coalition's periphery; certainly it lies beneath the fatuous claims bandied about by black spokespersons that the black constituency constitutes the Democrats' "core vote," as well as warnings that black support should not be taken for granted.[13] This perspective also illuminates a rational kernel within the "enthusiasm" rhetoric. Threats to withhold black support from the Democratic party cannot be made good, if only because the Republican program is thoroughly antagonistic to black interests; the specter of diminished enthusiasm therefore translates into reduction in elite efforts to mobilize voters on behalf of Democratic tickets.

Yet the challenge of Democratic instability exposes the potentially tragic limitations of the black elite's commitment to its narrowly instrumental orientation. The current debate over restructuring the Democratic party's priorities requires that claimant groups negotiate and affix themselves to comprehensive agendas that address fundamental issues of public policy, including positions on such matters as the appropriate framework and targets for ordering government economic policy (at national and local levels), the nature and scope of social welfare policy, and the direction of foreign and defense policies. Black leadership has responded to all these issues by conceding proposal of substantive arguments to other groups and has opted to join the debate in the main only to demand cosmetic black representation in administering whatever courses the party may take.

Two ramifications of that mode of response and the conceptual myopia from which it derives promise to exacerbate political elites' problems of efficacy and legitimacy in the black community. First, the absence of moorings in program or vision leaves political leadership aimlessly adrift in a sea of policy options, without the guidance of standards by which to negotiate among the various proposals emanating from others. Thus impaired in making critical judgments, black leadership compensates with a furtive opportunism that —given the prevalence of regressive alternatives in the present field of options—increases the likelihood of their alignment with strategies inimical to the interests of much of their black constituency. So, for example, the National Conference of Black Mayors at their April 1984 meeting endorsed the Reaganite stratagem of urban enterprise zones on the pretext of accommodation to *realpolitik*.[14]

The second ramification concerns the politically consequential choice of discursive terrain. Lacking any other basis, black elites have responded to current debates in a unidimensional language of racial entitlement. In so doing they inadvertently reinforce the rightist view that black concerns are peripheral, if not contrary, to the project of reconstructing a growth consensus. This language, which advances a notion of social obligation that is seemingly disconnected from a context of mutual civic responsibility, posits an incommensurate relation between blacks and the party's other interest configurations; when combined with the present cultural mood and traditional resistance to black-identified agendas, it is easily construed as antagonistic and weakens coalitional possibilities. This reductionist language of racial entitlement informed the Jackson phenomenon as well and helped to prevent integration of its claims regarding collective black self-fulfillment and its "Rainbow" pretensions. Moreover, this focus on racial entitlement in the Jackson campaign brought into relief its postures toward two other Democratic constituencies: labor and Jews.

Jackson, Blacks, and Labor—Troubled Allies

Practically from the first, Jackson defined the labor movement as an antagonist. The AFL-CIO's early and solid endorsement of Mondale very likely had much to do with Jackson's combative stance. He has, furthermore, a long history of criticizing labor as racist in its defense of seniority systems, support for military spending that arguably diverts funds from social programs, failure to develop black union leadership, and other matters.[15] Still, during the campaign Jackson adopted the rhetoric, propagated by Hart, Glenn, and the Republicans, that castigated the AFL-CIO as a nefarious "special interest" bent on hijacking the party and unfairly exercising its allegedly great and unaccountable power in pursuit of its own narrow gain. He consistently pitted black aspirations against labor's, contraposing the two groups as competitors for priority in the party's distributive queue.[16]

In focusing so closely on a race-specific set of concerns, Jackson's tack obscures an important fact about the relationship of Afro-Americans and organized labor. The AFL-CIO remains the strongest and most adamant voice pressing within the Democratic party for a policy agenda which emphasizes the social and economic welfare goals that benefit most of the black constituency. Indeed, labor's platform proposals far surpass Jackson's on a criterion of programmatic advancement of issues around which a "Rainbow Coalition" might solidify. Why, then, did Jackson single out labor as his bitterest adversary within the party? Two explanations are likely. One is that the narrowness of his political vision led him to cast the AFL-CIO's support for Mondale as a malevolent demonstration of hostility to black interests, which Jackson defined exclusively in relation to his attempt to increase his leverage in the Democratic coalition. The second explanation is more insidious, though not incompatible with the first. Jackson's attacks on the AFL-CIO as a "special interest" may be associated with the "corporate interventionist" strategy that he has helped to pioneer among race advocacy organizations.

Shortly before the 1984 presidential election Jackson's Operation PUSH, the NAACP, the African Methodist Episcopal Church's Western district, and several black trade and professional associations led a black and Hispanic defection from the boycott sponsored by the AFL-CIO of the Colorado-based Coors brewery company in exchange for the company's "pledge to redirect $625 million in investments into banks, publications and suppliers owned by black or Hispanic business executives." [17] The Colorado state AFL-CIO president bemoaned the defection from the "coalition of blacks, Hispanics, labor and church groups," suggesting that the black and Hispanic advocacy groups may have been responding to the Reaganite "economic climate." An NAACP official responded in defense that "it's just good business to do business with those who support you. Besides, it's not clear to me what labor's goal is. Some people at Coors feel it is to put them out of business." [18] As black leaders' racial agendas become ever more targeted to upper income, upper status black interests—as the focus of the "fair share agreements" exemplifies—the programmatic basis for unity with the labor movement's social agenda recedes.

Indeed, certification of racial status group arrangements for black managers and contractors does not disturb corporate labor or social practices at all. (Coors, for instance, incurs little monetary cost from its agreement.) This strategy easily could entail enlistment of black advocacy organizations actively on behalf of management against labor. Citing an instance close to home, while this manuscript was being written, the Yale University campus chapter of the NAACP sided with the university's administration against striking clerical and technical workers on the grounds that demonstration of loyalty could ensue in payoffs "down the line." Whichever explanation carries more weight, the fact that Jackson so comfortably latched onto the antilabor imagery presently in vogue indicates the potential for unscrupulousness that bedevils black elites' opportunistic conceptualization of politics.

7

Blacks and Jews in
the Democratic Coalition

⸻ ✳ ⸻ **T**he logic of Jackson's conflict with organized Jewry is more complex than his
hostility to labor because the political
connection between Afro-Americans and
Jews is more ambiguous. Recognition of this ambiguity is
limited by a ritualistic pattern of discussion of black/Jewish
relations that obscures the dynamics joining the groups. At
the nucleus of this discourse are the shibboleths that affirm
unity and proclaim a continuing history of common purpose.
Commitment to these shibboleths forces expressions of conflict into one of two modes: (1) oblique arguments couched
in terms of formal principles (for example, quotas) and ab-
stracted from the goals of Jews and blacks as historically specific social agents; or (2) an Aesopian criticism in which disagreement over issues that are structurally remote from the
groups' sphere of mutuality (for instance, the Middle East) is
adduced to stand for bases of tension closer to home. The path

to comprehending the structural foundations of alliance and dissension, both in general and as they were reflected through the Jackson phenomenon, requires breaking the delicately crafted ritual code and addressing squarely the practical substance of the black/Jewish dialectic in American politics.

Jews' Dual Status in Racial Dialogue

Certain points need to be made as a precondition for decoding. First, there is no simple "historic political relation between blacks and Jews." Instead, there have been several fields of political action in which fairly distinct congeries of Jews and blacks have mutually participated. Among these are Communist and other left-wing activity in the 1930s and 1940s, civil rights activism and its organizational elaboration into professionalized civil rights engineering, the national Democratic coalition, and its local articulations. With the exceptions of the radical Left (and to a slightly lesser extent grassroots civil rights activity) where "Jewishness" and/or "blackness" have been less significant as overtly institutionalized, official status categories, the Jewish/Afro-American relationship has been determined through the mediation of elite-driven formal advocacy organizations such as the NAACP and National Urban League on the one side and the American Jewish Congress, American Jewish Committee, and Anti-Defamation League of B'nai B'rith on the other.

Jewish elites have had at least two advantages in this mediated interaction. Because the interaction has been largely governed by an ideological commitment to interracialism, Jews have been able to steer "dialogue" from each side, both as representatives of autonomous Jewish interest groups and as prominent forces within interracial civil rights organizations. The peculiarity of Jewishness as a status that is neither racial, nor national nor, for that matter, necessarily religious exonerates Jewish elites from the imperative of organizational interracialism in their own domain while demanding obeisance to it from black civil rights organizations, as in the case of the black power elaboration out of the civil rights movement.[1] The double standard of this Jewish/black dialectic is so deeply ingrained that it generally does not surface for public observation and comment. However, a recent controversy may be illustrative.

In the early 1980s trustees of New York's famed Schomburg collection of Afro-Americana hired a curator who was white and rumored to be Jewish. Outraged black nationalists marched, demonstrated, and otherwise expressed anger and dismay at what they considered a travesty. Despite its origination from a rather crude and narrow-minded parochialism, the protest incisively brought the double standard into relief. While the idea of a Jewish Schomburg curator is plausible to the public consciousness, opponents observed, appointment of a black director of the Wiesenthal Center or a similar institution devoted to Jewish cultural documentation would seem somehow counterintuitive, if not plainly ludicrous. Notwithstanding the merits of the Schomburg case, which are very much open to debate, this incident exposes clearly one of the senses in which Jewish elites are advantageously situated in the "historic relation" with blacks; Jewish representation of black interests is legitimated by prevailing cultural norms while the notion of black custodianship of Jewish interests is not.

The second advantage redounding to Jews is related to the first. Black racial advocacy organizations depend largely on private philanthropy, access to which often runs through or can be vetoed by elites of Jewish interest organizations. Obviously, Jewish advocacy is not similarly constrained to placate black concerns. As a case in point, in the spring of 1976 I attended what amounted to a public job interview of Julian Bond, who recently had expressed an interest in succeeding Roy Wilkins as executive director of the NAACP. Bond, who from his Student Nonviolent Coordinating Committee days until that year had refrained from supporting Israeli policy in the

Middle East, had been invited to a "Meet the Press" forum at the Jewish Community Center in Atlanta. Although Bond finally had signed Bayard Rustin's annual Black Americans in Support of Israel Committee (BASIC) statement that year, he was apparently reluctant to attend what he suspected would be a grilling on the Middle East. According to a *Time* magazine reporter close to Bond and to the incident, Henry Lee Moon, an NAACP official, telephoned Bond and advised him very strongly of the need to attend the session if he were at all serious in his desire to replace Wilkins. He attended, and the tenor of the event approximated an inquisition or show trial, with some questioners explicitly characterizing Bond's attempt to maintain critical distance from Israel's interpretation of Middle East conflict as consequential for his NAACP aspirations. The reverse situation is unthinkable; black insistence on endorsement of affirmative action quotas or repudiation of Israel's ties to South Africa, for instance, never would be a pertinent criterion for organizational legitimation of Jewish leadership.

Black Leaders' Pragmatism toward Jews

Insofar as the relationship follows that pattern, the association of Jewish and black leadership is acted out on a terrain defined by the former. The hypothesis of commonality of interest therefore assumes the comparatively advantageous position occupied by Jewish organizational elites. This is not to suggest that blacks are duped, coopted, or coerced to pursue "Jewish interests." A more accurate view is that black and Jewish elites pursue their independent interests on the basis of pragmatic rationality that defines objectives within a given set of options. The apparent finitude of the options expresses acceptance of or acquiescence to an arrangement of social forces that constitutes the "rules of the game." [2] The elites' sphere of mutuality derives from their respective readings of possibilities afforded. The environmental condition of greater

Jewish institutional entrenchment combines with interracialism to structure a context of action in which rational, independent articulation and pursuit of pragmatic goals by black elites requires a nonreciprocal attentiveness to Jewish organizational interests.[3] The sacrosanct status of Israel in the Jewish agenda, for example, prohibits black elites' capacity to press their opposition to apartheid by criticizing the Israeli/South African axis. Despite the growth in the 1970s and 1980s of an elite-centered, Afro-American Africa lobby, organized Jewry's defensiveness concerning Israel limits public criticism among *black* leadership. Jewish Zionism, to put the matter somewhat provocatively, overrrides black Zionism— even in the black organizational apparatus!

The black elite agenda is organized according to a hierarchy of priorities in which, among other considerations, objectives that might engender opposition from Jewish organizations are treated as less important than those for which Jewish support or neutrality might be expected. (Continuing black support for quotas to achieve affirmative action goals appears to be an exception to this norm.) This hierarchy reinforces the notion of a special black/Jewish unity. The apparent convergence of black and Jewish elite interests, however, reflects a rational adaptation by blacks to a context in which the material costs of potential Jewish alienation are high. What makes for inequality in this sense—in addition to material dependency—is that black elites, because they do not similarly penetrate the core of Jewish strategic activity, cannot replicate the tacit (and sometimes not so tacit) veto power that Jewish elites have held in black interest articulation processes.

Obviously, the relative cost of loss of Jewish support is a function of the significance attached to that support in black leadership's strategic calculus, which is in turn dependent on the elite's particular perception of the range of acceptable options. To that extent, this situation ultimately is a symptom of black political elites' century-long pattern of uncritical acceptance of fundamental power relations in the general society and reliance on external sources of legitimation. However, the black/Jewish epicycle may contribute on its own as well to the Afro-American elite's crisis of political direction. Jewish representation on both sides of interracial dialogue not only has meant that an injunction to account for Jewish elite interests is embedded in black leadership's agenda-forming activity. The conceptual and discursive framework thus developed influences black political activity in two additional respects, with a single effect. On the one hand, elevation of interracialism to the status of a political principle—required to justify extrinsic intervention in agenda-setting—thoroughly conflates means and ends, goals, strategies, and tactics, and affirms a criterion for political debate that has little direct connection to public policy. On the other hand, because the programmatic basis for the unity of black and Jewish elites has become increasingly fragile, commonality can be vouchsafed only by restricting the scope of black political involvement as much as possible to a narrowly construed project of race relations engineering, or in the parlance of an earlier period, "race adjustment." Potential conflict is avoided by excluding certain areas of public policy from the realm of autonomous concern for black spokespersons. This restriction, of course, is consistent with the racial protest ideology that undergirds contemporary black politics anyway. The destabilization of the "historic unity" of black and Jewish elites since the civil rights era suggests that structural differentiation of the interests of their upper status and upwardly mobile constituencies may have reached a point at which mutuality cannot be assured even around the most incremental program of race relations management.

Distilled from the absurdly reified discourse of collective "hurt," "suffering," and "healing" through which it was voiced, the controversy between Jackson and Jewish elites says much about the present state of the "historic unity." Although Jackson's slurring references and links with Louis

Farrakhan created much furor, he had been viewed with considerable circumspection by Jewish elites from the beginning of his campaign.[4] Certainly, his history of association with the PLO and other Arab groups had much to do with Jewish wariness. Reaction to the "Hymie town" slurs, moreover, brought to light a series of anti-Semitic utterances made by Jackson in recent years.[5] Yet the Jackson camp's complaints that attacks on their candidate's insulting remarks were a smokescreen covering other objections, while hardly overcoming Jackson's culpability, have some basis.

Jackson's incidental remarks provoked a shrillness strikingly absent from reaction to the more programmatic and ideological anti-Semitism emanating from such quarters as the Moral Majority. In this regard, it is significant that Arthur Hertzberg, past president of the American Jewish Congress, has observed the spread of "revolt" against liberalism among middle class Jews motivated by a desire to "protect their class interest as 'haves.' " Hertzberg notes that this tendency extends even to toleration of "the emergence of a right-wing 'Christian America.' "[6]

Albert Vorspan, vice president of the Union of American Hebrew Congregations, indicated that he had rarely seen Jews so upset as they were over the Jackson controversy, and his explanation for the "deep dismay" also focused on material concerns. "For many Jews," Vorspan maintained, "this is an excuse to bolt concern for blacks, cities and the rest of it. For others, it will be an excuse to go for Ronald Reagan."[7] Although fears concerning widespread Jewish defection to Reagan were not realized, the material bases of black/Jewish tension remain intact.[8]

Status Displacement in Black/Jewish Conflict

Black/Jewish conflict springs from two main sources: (1) competition within the professional apparatus of social administration; and (2) black encroachment—via extension of the logic of affirmative action as an elite mobility strategy—on enclaves of relative Jewish privilege in education and elsewhere. Development of a community control orientation within black activism in the 1960s led to dramatic manifestation of the contraposition of blacks as clients of service agencies and institutions (for example, public schools) and Jews as professional service providers. This relation was overlapped by the tension between relatively entrenched Jews and upwardly mobile blacks seeking to carve out niches of their own in the public service apparatus. Of course, this class of objectives ultimately involved blacks and Jews only to the extent that they operated on that contested terrain, and the fundamental lines of cleavage where status-linked and structural rather than attitudinal.[9] However, the explosion surrounding the New York school crisis of 1967–68 set a precedent for redefining structurally generated conflict between blacks and Jews in terms purporting the rise of anti-Semitism among blacks.

The Ocean Hill–Brownsville controversy was the occasion of another instance of rare Jewish disturbance, and, as in the Jackson case, the frenzy was precipitated by charges of black anti-Semitism. The underlying substantive issue—conflict between the primarily black and Hispanic parents on one side and the primarily white teachers union over control of the recently decentralized Ocean Hill–Brownsville school district in Brooklyn[10]—was lost in the outcry. Albert Shanker, president of New York City's United Federation of Teachers, fought the impetus to community control, opposing the state's legislative provision for decentralization by describing it as "an attack on teachers" and raising the specter of "anti-Semitic conspiracy."[11] Thus the terms in which the mainly black parents had expressed a demand for participation were redefined and the nature of the debate altered.

Rabbi Jay Kaufmann, then executive director of B'nai B'rith, reduced the entire controversy to the significance of marginalia: an anti-Semitic leaflet, a child's anti-Semitic poem that had been read on the radio, and a handful of other, more vague horror stories. On this basis Kaufmann proclaimed "the prevalence and virulence of anti-Semitism presently festering in the Negro community," [12] and contended that there was "no question that the Negro community is ripe for a neo-fascism." [13] He acknowledged, almost in passing, the objective grounds of tension in Jewish visibility in administering black dispossession through the schools, public service apparatus, housing markets, and commercial infrastructure in the black community. [14] His proposals, however, were one-sided, calling on blacks to remember the extent to which their political interests have been connected with Jews'; more to the point, he chided black power–era blacks, instructively, for being "less willing than the youngsters of previous ethnic groups to demonstrate the patience required for the laborious, step-by-step ascent up the economic ladder [and] insisting that . . . their people be allowed to leapfrog over their peers and superiors into posts others are unwilling to abandon or forgo." [15] In this light Alan W. Miller, rabbi of the Society for the Advancement of Judaism, while denouncing the smattering of anti-Semitism around Ocean Hill–Brownsville as "the moronic lucubrations of illiterate racists," suspected that "those who are making the most noise about *black* anti-Semitism have a hidden agenda, a covert ideological bias." [16] He concluded from his experience as a parent in one of the schools affected by the teachers' strike against the community school board that "anti-Semitism was being used by Jews as part of a deliberate policy to unite New York Jews against the legitimate aspirations of black and Puerto Rican parents and children in a school system which has abysmally failed them." [17]

The "hidden agenda," then as now, was material interest. Albert Vorspan, who attempted both in 1968 and again in 1984 to project a voice of reason, asked: "Why is it that we Jews, who were not panicked by Wallace, Rockwell, Gerald L. K. Smith or the Ku Klux Klan, can be panicked by anti-Semi-

tism coming from blacks? And why is it that, when we talk
about anti-Semitism today, we talk about *black* anti-Semitism
almost exclusively?'' His answer was the same in 1969 as in
1984; the hysteria was an excuse ''to justify disengagement
and withdrawal from the social scene.''[18] Specifically in the
school issue, the agenda was ''manipulation of the Jewish
community by those who sought to line it up on one side (to
fight the 'black Nazis') in an economic dispute.''[19] While
joining in criticism of black leadership for not appearing
properly aggressive in denouncing expressions of anti-Semitism among blacks, Vorspan also noted the nearly complete
silence of Jewish spokespersons with regard to racist effu-
sions from the Jewish Defense League, striking teachers, and
others.[20] In so doing, he pointed to the core tension in the
Jewish/Afro-American relationship, which extends beyond the
issue of conflict in social service agencies—a conflict, he observed, that is to a considerable degree peculiar to New York
City. The broader and more enduring problem stems from the
double standard that has organized the groups' political interaction. As Vorspan said:

> The truth is that [black-Jewish relations] never were
> really good. We Jews did a great deal *for* black people,
> and that is precisely the point. We were the leaders, we
> called the shots, we set the timetable, we evolved the
> strategy, we produced the money . . . we were the supe-
> rior people. This was no relationship of peer to peer,
> equal to equal, powerful group to powerful group.[21]

Although Jews have been more visible than other whites in
support of black causes, this support has grown by no means
from altruism alone. Vorspan's 1969 characterization remains
persuasive:

> Jewish racial liberalism has operated in inverse relation to
> the distance from Jewish economic interests. Jewish orga-
> nizations were strong on desegregating the South; rela-

> tively few Jews were involved, and they were safely ig-
> nored. Jews supported fair housing and fair employment
> in the North; it was largely the WASP establishments
> which were cracked open, both for Jews and for blacks.
> Jewish organizations supported Lindsay's referendum for
> a civilian review board in New York City, that was di-
> rected against Irish cops. But the school strike impinged
> upon large number of Jews. . . . Jews have become a
> successful part of the American system. . . . They will
> resist efforts to smash [it], to restructure it fundamentally,
> or to "sacrifice Jewish interests" in the process of re-
> form.[22]

While not belittling the extent to which Jewish individuals have
come together with blacks around honestly shared commitment to positions of democratic principle, it is necessary to
recognize that the black/Jewish nexus has benefited Jews also
by enabling them to mobilize black support for agendas that
advance Jewish interests. As black elites' interests uncouple
from Jews', the foundation of the general alliance becomes
unsteady.

The fight against discrimination in higher education, restricted housing covenants, and the like aided Jews as much
as blacks—if not more, given the Jews' relatively better position to realize the benefits of strict equality of opportunity.
The demand that old-boy admissions standards at elite universities be replaced by a "meritocratic" principle based on
"objective" criteria such as standardized tests has worked
doubly to Jews' advantage, by eliminating the nefarious practice of maintaining quotas on Jewish admissions and by advocating the adoption of a standard of intelligence or capacity
demonstrated by the test operations that Jewish applicants
typically perform well. In this sense, Anglo-Saxon wealth and
its cultural and stylistic attributes were the "meritocratic"
criteria used by the entrenched old-boy crowd to deny access

to other claimant groups, including Jews and the unwashed. Performance on "objective" Scholastic Aptitude Tests (SATs) became the compensatory affirmative action vehicle allowing Jews to overcome their "isolation" from WASP, old-boy networks. Generalization of "objective" testable standards of capacity—for university admissions, civil service employment, professional certification, and so on—both expands and constricts access simultaneously. On the one hand, it limits access by narrowing selection to a one-dimensional criterion, the ablility to perform certain mensurable operations (largely involving quick recall) in a particular kind of controlled context. This criterion undoubtedly approaches a notion of capacity that is more inclusive, more compatible with the values of intellectual subculture, and more tolerable to the democratic temper than is assignment of privilege on the basis of unmediated reference to ascriptive characteristics. After all, though SATs and Graduate Record Exams are hardly flawless predictors of performance, they nonetheless can be useful in identifying certain strengths and weaknesses that may influence academic performance. (The utility of standardized exams for mail carriers, firefighters, and social workers, of course, is more dubious.) However, since it tends to restrict definition of merit to ability to complete a specified range of abstract mental performances, that impersonalized standard discounts other attributes that might equally be valuable as indicators of capability or, for that matter, as components of a definition of the goals of education or of a given profession. Put another way, selection of one or another criterion of ability to perform in a role is premised on a prior assumption concerning the proper composition of the role; such assumptions entail specific views regarding social utility and are to that extent political choices.

In the old-boy view of elite education, for example, access is governed by a goal of socialization directed toward securing transgenerational reproduction of a cohesive upper-class culture. Therefore, correct breeding is a standard of "merit" because it is a functional requirement for participation in advanced socialization processes whose intended outcome is production of well-rounded members of an elite. The attack on this restrictiveness conducted from below in the name of equality of opportunity demands opening of access to groups incapable of satisfying requirements of pedigree and thus proposes an amendment to the functional definition of elite education. The more "objective" standard of test-brightness represents a compromise that mediates the breeding requirement—though in principle more than fact—by installing a criterion which, while protecting entrenched elites' access through the prep school network, is oriented to producing test-brightness and technically is accessible to those who have assimilated the skill by other means. At the same time, this opening—which is at any rate qualified—is accompanied by a functional redefinition of the educational project that tends to reduce it to completion of a series of discrete, finely measured performances. The goal of multifarious socialization, that is, is deemphasized by the objectivistic criterion.

The point of this excursus is simply that the practical notion of meritocratic standards that has been taken to fulfill equality of opportunity ideology is neither intrinsically more inviolable nor necessarily freer of bias than that which it replaces or any other. Recognition of its partiality in turn repoliticizes the specific programmatic basis of black/Jewish tension that has developed in the post–civil rights era. At the time of the Ocean Hill–Brownsville controversy even Miller and Vorspan opposed the developing orientation among black elites to shift from formal equality of opportunity to equality of outcome as a focus of antidiscrimination activity. (Vorspan, at least, seems subsequently to have retreated from his opposition.) Other, less sympathetic Jewish elite spokespersons laid down an unequivocal anti–affirmative action line, supported by old bromides to the effect that blacks should be content in their place in the queue of ethnic succession and follow in the footsteps of other groups—specifically Jews—while waiting their turn. There is no need to rehearse the various arguments concerning the propriety of or need for affirmative action strategies. Regardless of their efficacy or lack thereof, the important fact is that those strategies are understood by Jewish elites as infringements on norms for allocation of privilege from which they benefit and which they interpret as rights. This, then, is the substantive basis of black/Jewish conflict in the current period.

Jesse Jackson's simple-minded anti-Semitic discourse, which on one occasion at least he projected as "talking black," reflects his opportunistic appropriation of the outlook of an upwardly mobile but harried stratum in the black community, a stratum which—like Kafka's burrowing animal—is consumed by fearful visions of antagonists pressing from all sides. This outlook yields a meanness of spirit and small-mindedness that historically have opened to protofascistic articulations in Europe, Latin America, and elsewhere.

Certainly, the cathartic frenzy that Jackson cultivated, with its elimination of debate among Afro-Americans, reveals the dangerous tendencies inherent in that mind-set. As William Raspberry observed after the obious "Hymie" incident, Jackson ruined the one contribution that he might have made to national political debate during the primary season, that is, the call for a more reasonable approach to United States policy on the Middle East.[23] In one stroke Jackson sacrificed the moral authority on which he might have stood to demand a Middle Eastern policy that acknowledges the legitimacy of interests other than Israel's. However, in an environment in which the American Zionist lobby is disposed to brand any criticism of Israel as anti-Semitism, Jackson's slurs not only tainted his image; they also destroyed—albeit unfairly—the credibility of the stance with which he had aligned himself.

Yet neither Jackson's offensive remarks nor his association with a critical posture toward Israel can account for the intensity of Jewish elites' reaction and the proliferation of accusations of black anti-Semitism. Similar or worse slurs by others—for example, the Southern Baptist Convention president's blunt assertion that God will not answer the prayers of a Jew, or James Watt's occasional epithets—have failed to elicit comparably strident reactions.

The source of the caterwauling over Jackson is the same "hidden agenda" that Rabbi Miller sensed in the Ocean Hill–Brownsville controversy. The anti-Jackson diatribe was expressed consistently on three levels: two emotional and hysterical, one calm and programmatic. Most overt was castigation of his anti-Semitic statements and his link to Farrakhan. Then his association with Arafat and receipt of Arab money simultaneously reinforced the image of black support of genocide against Jews *and* the notion that criticism of Israel equals anti-Semitism. Finally, and invariably, came reaffirmation of Jewish opposition to affirmative action quotas. The three were tied together neatly, and—in line with the 1968–69 experience—it was the last that was the substantive issue. At the height of the Jackson controversy, Charles Wittenstein of the Anti-Defamation League volunteered that "we don't think a racial quota is ever benign because, while conferring a benefit on one race, it imposes a disability on another."[24] Vorspan intimated that affirmative action lay at the crux of the problem when, at a forum organized to quell tension, he acknowledged that he was "deeply troubled by those who are so insensitive to . . . black needs that they turn affirmative action into a black-Jewish confrontation, which it never must be."[25]

It is in this context that the brutally adamant line taken on Jackson by Jewish elites around the Democratic convention should be perceived. It was at the same time that Jackson was pressing his anemic platform—which included endorsement of affirmative action quotas—that Jewish spokespersons insisted most strongly that Mondale repudiate him as the price for Jewish support.[26] Even after Jackson's plea for forgiveness in his convention address, spokespersons from the Anti-Defamation League (ADL), American Jewish Congress, American Jewish Committee, and Synagogue Council of America remained aloof. Nathan Perlmutter, director of the ADL, in fact escalated his requirements of Jackson on the spot to include repudiation of Castro and the Sandinistas as "echo chambers of Anti-Zionism and anti-Americanism."[27] (It was not clear, however, on what basis the ADL claimed authority to define and protect "Americanism" from other citizens.) It is difficult in this light to resist the argument that the furor about Jackson's anti-Semitism conceals a more immediately programmatic alienation. Vorspan's question of 1969 answers as much in this regard as it asks: "If special provisions are made to bring black youngsters into universities, should Jews convert the issue into one of anti-Semitism on the ground that such quotas would, in practice, lessen the opportunities of some Jewish youngsters to be judged on individual merit alone?"[28]

What all this means is that the political relationship between blacks and Jews is ambiguous, within the Democratic party and otherwise. To the extent that there is reason behind concerns expressed by Hertzberg and others that Jewish elites are poised to bolt from the party's liberal wing, that relationship becomes even less precise. Clarification is possible, but it requires fulfillment of two conditions. First, it is necessary to discard the shibboleths of special unity. That unity is an ideological fiction, a product of the circumstance that Jewish elites have dominated discussion of the black/Jewish nexus. As Rabbi Miller observed, "In the absence of a black Anti-Defamation League, anti-black remarks by Jews have rarely received the same publicity as anti-Semitic remarks by blacks."[29] In the past Jews and blacks have been joined spo-

radically in pursuit of common or compatible agendas; even
then compatibility often has been exaggerated by the skewed
character of the union. Jews do not appear to be significantly
different from other white groups in their attitudes and behavior toward Afro-Americans. Cruse expresses a broader black
opinion in contending that

> American Negroes have, in deference to Jewish sensibili-
> ties, tolerated Jewish ambivalence, Jewish liberalism,
> Jewish paternalism, Jewish exploitation, Jewish racism,
> Jewish radicalism, Jewish nationalism, in the same way
> in which they have lived with similar attributes in the
> white Anglo-Saxon.[30]

Once that empty ideological baggage is jettisoned, it will
be possible to satisfy the second condition for clarification of
the Jewish/Black political relation: comparison of Afro-
American and Jewish leadership's independently articulated
agendas for a programmatic consensus within American politics in general and the Democratic party in particular. Dialogue and debate over those agendas, within the party as a
forum, will clarify the political directions and visions of the
future of the polity with which the two groups identify and
will in the process resolve the issues pertaining to their capacity for concerted action.

With respect to this project, the Jackson phenomenon is an
emblem of the broader failure of the black political elite. Not
only was Jackson's initiative itself bereft of vision or program; it was possible to conduct such an enterprise only because the spokesmanship stratum, of which Jackson was a part,
has generated no programmatic discourse that is sensitive to
the structural environment in which the Afro-American population (especially the black poor) is embedded. In a context
in which, since 1980 at least, the value of the Democratic
party's commitment to its liberal constituency has been increasingly assailed from within,[31] the absence of a coherent

black agenda tends to forfeit leverage to Democratic neocon-servatives who favor driving blacks to the coalition's periph-ery. Ironically, while the Jackson campaign claimed just the opposite intention, its effect was to take blacks out of the mainstream of the important debate over the party's future—all the more because the Jackson forces could find no position to press other than the right to be accounted for properly in the party hierarchy.

8

The Media, the Left, and the Jackson Campaign

Jackson's rise to prominence in 1984 was fueled by a number of factors; central among them were his impressive knack for self-promotion and the dispirited and uncertain conditions prevailing within the Afro-American population. However, the relation between the Jackson campaign phenomenon and its black constituency was catalyzed by the functional intervention of the mass media, which authorized the candidate's claims of a popular groundswell on his behalf by reproducing them uncritically. Although Jackson's subsequent actions and statements were scrutinized more closely, the essential assertion that legitimized his effort—that he held the proxies of the "black masses"—was accepted on its face by major print and broadcast media from the first. In addition, the white Left, though it offered some criticism, was largely neutralized by the campaign's projected imagery of a mass movement of the dispossessed. The treatment the campaign received from those two quarters illustrates certain fundamental problems, both conceptual and ideological, that influence the way in which politics among Afro-Americans is understood outside the black community. Because of the persisting importance of external mechanisms of elite legitimation, moreover, those problems affect the terms of strategic political discourse within the black population as well.

Jackson, the National Media, and Black Political Celebrity

Early television coverage of Jackson's initiative broadcast without qualification his carefully devised performances before crowded churches and black college auditoriums—evocative of civil rights/black power era coverage of King and Stokely Carmichael—and validated his premise that "the black masses" propelled his candidacy. The *New York Times* beatified Jackson's claim by noting that, despite lack of enthusiasm from the "black leadership family," Jackson "took his cue from revivalistic rallies conducted all around the country to the chant of 'Run, Jesse, run.' "[1] Throughout the primary season network television and the national press repeated the formula that identified Jackson's campaign as the all-encompassing black concern in the presidential selection process. By the time of the Democratic convention, public discourse concerning Afro-American representation in the party's preparation for the November election had been largely subsumed into the issue of negotiation of a package of practical and symbolic payoffs that could secure Jackson's support for a Mondale-led ticket. Thus the media anointed Jackson's attempt to gain paramountcy as a black spokesperson.

In this context the candidate's complaints of unfair treatment in the media appear curious. In part they derive from the distinctive style of his self-assertion as a black leader. Since his emergence after King's death as a visible personality in protest elite circles, Jackson has expended great effort in cultivating reporters as a means to political celebrity. Observers of his career have noted that he consistently has sought attention from media representatives, alternating cajolery with charges of victimization by those who have not been properly supportive of his efforts.[2] Notwithstanding his protests, the fact remains—as conservative columnist Pat Buchanan replied to a lamenting Jackson—that he received more extensive coverage than did Glenn, Hollings, or other candidates with similarly marginal performances in early primaries. Moreover, his campaign was treated as a "serious" candidacy even after it was clear that he had no chance either to win nomination or to affect designation of the nominee. This circumstance begs explanation, and an element of that explanation lies in the peculiar orientation of news media to the black community.

Les Payne pointed toward the basis of that relationship when he said that the media "focused on Jackson more as a historical figure than as a serious presidential candidate."[3] Continual proclamation of Jackson's effort as "historic" and rehearsal of his slogan of running for "respect" as the purpose of the campaign reflect a disposition within the media to siphon off the actions of black agents from the mainstream of American political discourse and to neatly categorize them under the rubric *"black* politics" or *"black* agenda." This disposition appears on many levels, ranging from the typical practice among local media of—in the words of a colleague and former professor—"reporting the black community from the police blotter" to Marvin Kalb's insistence that Jackson clarify on the "Meet the Press" television program whether he was a "black man who happens to be an American running for the presidency . . . or . . . an American who happens to be a black man running for the presidency."[4] Though not necessarily the conscious intention of individual reporters or their employers, the outcome of this approach—which betrays the persisting assumption that a narrowly defined category of race relations exhausts the realm of Afro-Americans' appropriate concern in the polity—was to sanction a pattern of public debate over national priorities in the 1984 campaign season that ghettoized black interests.

One might object that because the media are relatively neutral arenas for public discussion, the real sources of ghettoization of blacks in public policy debate must be sought elsewhere. Indeed, as I have argued, black leadership strata have failed to develop policy agendas in the present period and therefore have rendered themselves mute in current debate.[5] The relative neutrality of the media is an issue very much open to question;[6] it is not necessary to resolve that question, however, to conclude that coverage of the Jackson phenomenon reinforced a ghettoized view of Afro-Americans' political objectives. In fact, as the media, by acquiescence, gave a cultural imprimatur to Jackson's allegation that his initiative was identical with the race's collective aspirations, black leadership responded as cue-takers, embracing a terminology which accepted that interpretation.

Clearly, Jackson was not immune from criticism in the print and broadcast media; the recurring bugbear of his anti-Semitic remarks and his mercurial behavior during and after the Democratic convention, as well as his international activities, occasioned critical—sometimes caustic—commentary. Yet the fundamental and most dubious claim that he made, that is, that he was the individual repository of the racial voice, went unchallenged. A minimal explanation for the credulousness implicit in that silence is that it derives from familiar and commonly held assumptions that standard principles of political representation do not apply among Afro-Americans. Although Jackson's campaign technically was for Democratic nomination for the United States presidency in 1984, the orthodox media tacitly colluded with his exaggerated contention that he was running to be recognized as paramount national black spokesman, an office for which no election ever has been held. Responsible for this tacit journalistic collusion are three connected presuppositions that have structured perception of black political life outside the black community for a century: (1) black people have little authentic stake as such in the political community apart from matters that explicitly concern race; (2) blacks constitute a special collectivity on the margins of the polity, for whom procedural mechanisms of leadership selection are not particularly relevant; and (3) the political opinions, needs, and desires of Afro-Americans are opaque to outsiders except insofar as they are crystallized in the agenda of a generic racial spokesperson.

Journalists' natural adherence to those presuppositions converged with the rationale of organic leadership on which Jackson grounded his ambitions, and as a result black participation in 1984 presidential politics was diverted onto a side track. Thus the *New York Times,* at a point when it was unequivocally certain that the candidate could have no impact on the convention's outcome, effusively proclaimed Jackson victorious.[7] That proclamation was possible—profuse rhetoric about a "first 'serious' black presidential candidacy" aside—precisely because Jackson's effort was *not* taken seriously as a campaign for the Democratic nomination. Nor could it have been so taken by any reasonable observer; there never was any possibility that Jackson would win the nomination, and it was incontrovertibly clear by no later than the Illinois primary that he could not garner enough delegate votes to influence the nomination. Jackson's flair for news-worthiness combined with the media's acceptance of a ghettoizing premise to provide the buoyancy that kept his campaign afloat as a major topic for public attention.

In some cases the ease with which the media acknowledged Jackson as the new principal black leader derived not merely from outlooks that were inaccurate, myopic, or patronizing; more strategic motivations may have operated as well. The thesis that Jackson had ascended to primacy among black leaders was instrumentally useful to commentators for whom questioning the legitimacy of entrenched black political elites was an element of a broader challenge to the efficacy of liberal agendas. Frederick Allen, political editor of the *Atlantic Constitution,* asserted that ''Jackson's explosion into the role of premier black leader in the country is indisputable.''[8] However, Allen's elevation of Jackson was accompanied by an obverse contention that ''Atlanta's black leaders, like their counterparts across the country, have no earthly idea where their people are going'' and a heavy implication that black leaders identified with Mondale had been discredited among their constituents.[9] Joseph Perkins of the *Wall Street Journal* shortly before the November elections expatiated at considerable length about the alleged ''incongruity of [black leaders' liberal] public postures and the feelings of their constituencies.''[10]

Moreover, as one strain of media reaction suggests, the proposition of Jackson's prominence resuscitated an older practice of deflecting racial aspirations by tying them to the prospects of a putatively central leader. Appeals to the latter to proceed with moderation, guided by the instrumental rationality required to advance a political career, constitute instructions in racial strategy. The *Atlanta Journal,* for example, exhorted Jackson to desist from making ''pie-in-the-sky promises'' to his followers who ''have been exluded from the American mainstream . . . [and therefore] . . . have less understanding of the institutional and practical limitations on any office-holder.'' The *Journal*'s fear was that inflated promises could deepen the alienation of those constituents, many of whom ''are already resentful of the establishment.''[11] The *Journal*'s counsel was only more explicit than other expressions of concern that Jackson act ''responsibly'' in the position of leadership primacy that he was held to have won. Black spokespersons such as Fauntroy and Wilkins—

who only recently had repudiated the notion of unitary black leadership—fueled this view inadvertently by their assent in Jackson's claims to paramountcy.

The Campaign and the Left: Elevation of Form over Substance

For its part, the Left generally did not demonstrate greater reflectiveness than more orthodox media in its treatment of Jackson's candidacy. On campuses and in leftist periodicals the campaign generated enthusiastic support and motion. Barry Commoner reminded readers that "while Mr. Jackson has been making news he is also making history." [12] Philip Green first judged the Jackson campaign to be the most promising political effort "in a half-century." [13] Then, in replying to Paul Berman's rather defensive but not entirely unsound criticism of the candidate,[14] Green recycled the campaign's warning that Jackson had to be "respected enough at the convention to encourage him to turn out [the black] vote for whoever the Democratic nominee may be." Acknowledging the possibility that Jackson may well have been only an ordinary, opportunistic politician and not a "true left-winger," Green proclaimed the mythical "Rainbow" as an entity separable from and more important than Jackson's character and political integrity.[15] In lamenting that the "Rainbow Coalition is declining into a movement for blacks only" and assigning "much of the responsibility for the decline" to whites, Green simply repeated the campaign's fiction that there had been such a coalition in the first place.[16]

Andrew Kopkind expressed perhaps the most ebullient extreme of Jackson's support within the Left. Identifying the campaign as representative of a purportedly "quickening black movement," Kopkind linked the Jackson phenomenon with, *among other things,* the "triumphal images of Chicago's Mayor Harold Washington, Philadelphia's Mayor Wilson Goode . . .

the suggestive sight of caravans rumbling through Southern hamlets and Northern ghettos on voter registration drives . . . [and] a rush of new symbols: a black Miss America, a black police commissioner for New York City, a black astronaut."[17] He went on, in an effusion of empty sentimentality that displayed a startling historical amnesia, to imbue Jackson's effort and black electoral activity in general with a "special spiritual force" and to chide less enthusiastic liberals, leftists, and others for their hesitance.[18] He rebutted charges that the campaign had no clear, substantive policy program by diminishing the importance of "careful weighing of 'the issues' " and defending Jackson's apparent choice "to project an aura of power rather than to distribute an endless stream of position papers."[19] And he discounted the weight of criticism of Jackson's gambit from other black political spokespersons by noting that they—presumably unlike Jackson—"owe their status and power to white liberals and the Democratic Party."[20]

While Jackson's opponents within the black political elite certainly derived legitimations from outside the black community, they were hardly less authentic (or inauthentic) in that regard than the candidate himself. In fact, with the exception of Coretta Scott King, each of the critics named by Kopkind regularly satisfied an empirical criterion of legitimation among his *black* constituents that never validated Jackson's claims—electoral accountability. By contrast, Jackson, who was no less integrated into political elite circles than his critics, had to demonstrate his claims to authenticity only to corporate sponsors and government or philanthropic grantors, without any formal intervention by a palpable black constituency. As I have argued in chapter 3, obviation of the requirement to ratify leadership claims within the black community is a characteristic of the protest elite cohort of which Jackson, like Mrs. King, was a representative. An outcropping of their style of unmediated negotiation with white elites has been the devel-

opment of the "corporate interventionist" racial strategy—led by Jesse Jackson—that is structurally removed from the domain of public discourse and articulates an exceedingly narrow, self-serving elite agenda, hardly in line with the programmatic orientation of the Left. Kopkind's enthusiasm—which in all fairness captures an extreme within the Left—may well have blinded him to the inconsistencies and anomalies embedded in his view of Jackson's effort. However, the inadequacy of his interpretation also reflects much deeper problems regarding the place of the black community in the purview of the Left in general. These problems ultimately proceed from assumptions about black political life very similar to those which I have described in relation to the news media.

At least four factors can account for the tendency within the Left to misinterpret Jackson's initiative as the well-spring of an emancipatory political movement. First is wishful thinking. The Left had endured a decade-long winter of apparent social quiescence, and the prospect of Reagan's reelection no doubt made their political isolation seem yet more acute. Desperation often leads to clutching at straws, and in the present context an initiative that clothes itself in the symbolic attire of a transformative social movement is likely to generate visceral acceptance from the desperate and isolated. Jackson's choice to adorn himself in the raiments of civil rights activism undoubtedly accounts for a significant measure of his support among those who identify with left-wing politics. The prolonged absence of critical political movement on the Left very likely engendered a cultural "forgetting" of what actually constitutes such a movement. As Marx once remarked concerning John Stuart Mill, "On the level plain, simple mounds look like hills"; in this case, however, the desire to envisage a variegated terrain obscures the fact that even the mound is a mirage.

Second, Jackson's candidacy appeared to some to open an avenue through which leverage for their discrete agendas could be enhanced within the Democratic party or other influential circles. Roger Wilkins, of the Institute for Policy Studies, in his flamboyant panegyric for Jackson provides an insight in this regard. Arguing that the candidate could become "the politician who will finally provide the coherent post–New Deal definition that the Left and the Democratic party have been seeking so desperately," Wilkins disclosed an instrumental basis for leftist support of the "Rainbow." The campaign had attracted "a range of thinkers and activists who found [Jackson] to be an enormously effective vehicle for getting their ideas before the public."[21] The vision of systemic access and influence easily could overshadow the ambiguities surrounding the campaign's various claims, all the more in the bleak environment for the Left that Reaganism's success had created. I do not mean to suggest that this instrumental mediation is necessarily ignoble; on the contrary, political association grounded on convergence of autonomous interests and objectives constitutes the most honest and trustworthy basis for affiliation in contemporary politics. However, in the dialectic of the Jackson initiative and its advocates on the Left, the latter's independent interestedness is troublesome because—by enabling support for reasons that were extrinsic to Jackson's claims—it helped to impede critical reflection on the campaign.

A third factor is rooted in part in the antinomical images that the campaign projected. While Jackson based his effort in the black community on slogans of empowerment ("It's our turn now") and emotional appeals, his approach to white audiences attended more to programmatic positions. Even though those programmatic utterances were generally so superficial as to elicit Reston's observation that they could "fit onto a bumper sticker," Jackson's genuflection toward broad principles of the Left's agenda—opposition to United States policy in Central America, reductions in military spending, and so on—posed an attractive alternative to the other Democratic candidates, who tilted toward Reagan's stance to prove their anticommunist patriotism. At the same time, the symbolic morsels that the campaign tossed leftward deflected attention from its failure to develop policy proposals that addressed the particular interests of the main constituency that it claimed to represent, the Afro-American population.[22] The public policy agenda that Jackson took to the convention's platform negotiations reflects the relative importance that his initiative assigned to the white Left and black audiences. Of the four planks that he proposed, two—reduction in military spending and nonintervention in Central America—were prominent concerns of his white audience, while the only one of the four that had any currency in the black community was the call for more affirmative action, and even that scarcely qualifies as a burning issue universally among Afro-Americans.

Finally, the naivete shown by much of the Left relative to the Jackson phenomenon grew also from a chronic superficiality that tends to characterize leftist—as well as other white—perceptions of politics and life in general among Afro-Americans. Because it informs the ways that the black community figures into the American political landscape, moreover, this tendency cuts across the other three factors as well. A simplistic view of the dynamics that structure Afro-American political behavior facilitates acceptance of unwarranted claims as a matter of course. Indeed, dispositions to mistake the campaign for the coming of a long-awaited movement, to inflate its significance because of its potential instrumentality for other purposes, and to gloss the antinomical character of its appeals to black and white audiences cannot be considered entirely apart from the impact of assumptions that render black political activity either opaque or uninteresting as an object for critical scrutiny.

Two core assumptions about the relation of blacks to the American polity, which initially appear to be diametrically opposed, converge ultimately around a devaluation of the need for careful examination of Afro-American politics as a historically specific element of the national political culture. On the one hand are the exceptionalist presuppositions that I have described in relation to the media's treatment of Jackson, and elsewhere in this volume. These reduce to a premise that the black community is peripheral both to certain norms of political organization and behavior (for example, participation and leadership selection by means of formal democratic representation) and to standards of political interpretation and judgment otherwise applied. This premise, which amounts to a form of racial condescension, uncouples discussion of black political activity from consideration of the behavioral and normative maincurrents of American politics: it assumes the former to proceed from idiosyncratic structuring principles, to be an exotic appendage to the body politic. Little basis or incentive exists, therefore, for observation of dissonance or anomaly between appearance and reality, statement and fact in the black community.

On the other hand is a view that mechanically collapses black political activity into universal—and therefore Procrustean—models of ethnic political development in the United States. Ironically, this interpretation, beneath its ostensibly homogenizing aspirations, also rests on a fundamentally exceptionalist perspective that approaches Afro-American politics as an ersatz form of general patterns of ethnic interest-group development. The civil rights movement, black power radicalism, and the protest leadership style thus appear less as products of discrete circumstances operating in and on the black population than as marginal deviations from putatively normal processes.[23] In both cases exceptionalist assumptions separate explanation of black politics from a need to examine the endemic characteristics—such as patterns of cleavage, nature of political argument, and styles of legitimation—that mediate the black community's structural integration into the polity.

Chronic Problems in the Left's Orientation toward Blacks

The Left has shown itself repeatedly over several decades not to be immune from either the tendency toward analytical superficiality regarding blacks or its undergirding exceptionalist premises. Harold Cruse discussed this problem at great length in the late 1960s in the context of the interaction of blacks and other groups in the organized Marxist Left, with particular attention to issues of instrumentalization and custodianship of the "Negro Question."[24] Richard Wright and Ralph Ellison also addressed eloquently, in their fiction as well as in critical essays, the naivete and opportunism which often governed the Left's relation to blacks between the New Deal and the civil rights era.[25] Ellison was especially explicit in his criticism of versions of the exceptionalist premise that have appeared within the Left, and he noted acutely the paternalism and interpretive vapidness that can ensue from suspension of critical standards in discussion of Afro-American affairs. His assessment was trenchant:

Many of those who write of Negro life today seem to assume that as long as their hearts are in the right place they can be as arbitrary as they wish in their formulations. Others seem to feel that they can air with impunity their most private Freudian fantasies as long as they are given the slightest camouflage of intellectuality and projected as "Negro." They have made of the no-man's land created by segregation a territory for infantile self-expression and intellectual anarchy. They write as though Negro life exists only in light of their belated regard, and they publish interpretations of Negro experience which would not hold true for their own or for any other form of human life.[26]

The problem that Ellison described is by no means unique to, or even most prevalent among, Leftists. Yet the tendency toward exceptionalism has exerted a continuing influence on the Left's approach to the black population. Exaltation of an idealized view of black folk life and its alleged organicism—most distinctive prior to the "revolutionary" turn during the civil rights era—connects with New Left counterculturists' imagery of blacks as the embodiment of a more visceral and authentic humanity, with the Students for a Democratic Society's facile identification with the Black Panther Party and the "Third Worldist" mythology of the black-revolutionary-as-urban-guerrilla, and with more recent ingenuousness concerning the rise of black officialdom. This kind of exceptionalist view of the black community underlies Kopkind's charge that the Jackson campaign's critics in the Left were unappreciative that "Black funk is maddeningly different from left funk,"[27] as well as his implication that a campaign for the presidency and the Miss America pageant are somehow commensurable arenas for black aspiration. Again, Kopkind's argument is extreme, but it differs from more typical perspectives in degree rather than in kind.

The tracings of exceptionalism are visible in other contexts as well. Respectable leftist journals habitually bracket their intellectual integrity when considering contributions pertaining to Afro-Americans. An editor of a journal that had published one such piece acknowledged, when confronted, that the article was at best second-rate. His defense was that the journal needed to publish *something* on blacks, and the admittedly weak manuscript was the only one that had come along. Similarly, in the late 1970s the founder of a then fledgling left-wing press expressed reluctance at considering a manuscript that included critical assessments of the outcomes of black protest activity. His concern was that although the press had not yet published any manuscripts by "black authors," it very much wanted to do so, and he feared that an initial offering which might be read in any way as a "negative" statement would create an unfavorable impression.

These instances, and the general outlook they represent, reflect in part a racial defensiveness that has been generated in the Left by the ambivalent signals projected from blacks in the post–black power period. Black activists, after all, frequently have challenged the rights of white leftists to make critical judgments concerning Afro-American affairs. However, the presumption that idiosyncratic standards of political conduct apply in the black community worsens—or possibly even creates—this difficulty by undermining the basis for considered discrimination among claims made by blacks. As the attitude of the abovementioned publisher indicates, this defensiveness fuels an aversion within the Left to controversy among Afro-Americans. At the same time, aversion to controversy is logically grounded in exceptionalist premises. The black community's presumed marginality to normal political discourse eliminates the means for comprehending debate among blacks, while persisting assumptions of Afro-American organicism and attitudinal uniformity prompt a desire to locate a single, "authentic" black point of view. Defensiveness thus reinforces a troublesome tendency to accept superficially articulate black individuals who will associate with the Left as generic racial spokespersons.[28] This results in authorization of an orthodoxy on discourse about Afro-Americans without consideration of either the ambiguities and complexity of political dynamics within the black community or the actual linkages of designated spokespersons to bases of legitimacy and support among blacks.

Lack of skepticism regarding Jackson's initiative was in this sense symptomatic of an inclination within the Left (as in the media and in the culture in general) to remove discussion of Afro-American political activity from its constitutive context, that is, the dynamic of cleavage and interest aggregation within the black population and its articulation through the American polity and its state processes. This separation, moreover, is justified by the ironic premise that generally operative patterns and norms of political behavior are inapplicable in the black community. Rather than prodding investigation of a suggestive anomaly, as one might expect, this premise—in positing an *intrinsic* difference—hypostatizes the distinctive features of the political dynamics at work among blacks in abstracto and shunts them off to the periphery of political life.

Consequently, political discussion about blacks proceeds on a basis that does not attend to vital issues of political practice within the black population. These include, but are not limited to, the following: (1) the nature of representation and criteria of legitimacy; (2) the strengths and limitations of electoral politics and its relation to other mechanisms for racial advocacy; (3) constraints that affect formulation of racial agendas; (4) the normative and institutional foundations for popular political action in the black community; and (5) the impact of intraracial stratification on the purposive orientation of black politics. Without addressing these issues—each of which has both a historical and an empirical dimension—there is little likelihood of escape from the crises of purpose and understanding within which Afro-American politics presently is mired. My hope is that this volume has demonstrated the importance of attending to these issues, which can attain clarity and contingent resolution only through practical activity and critical discourse. This is the real, albeit inadvertent, significance of the Jackson phenomenon. Because of its celebrity status, it crystallized in a highly visible fashion both the contexts and the immediate terms of the political crisis that it reproduced. By fomenting and projecting an unambiguously false image of a popular, emancipatory Afro-American politics, the Jackson campaign hinted negatively at factors and conditions for which such a politics must account.

Epilogue: Prospects and Proposals for Emancipatory Interests

The analysis and arguments that I have presented here may raise more questions than they resolve concerning politics among Afro-Americans in the current situation. If so, that is as it should be, since my major intention in writing this book was to stimulate (and, I hope, to reorient) inquiry and debate. In that context, raising questions is as important as answering them. However, there are two issues that remain to be clarified, lest they create unwarranted confusion over this book's implications and assumptions. These issues are whether elected officials now should be seen as "true" representatives of black political interests, and what an appropriate emancipatory black political strategy would entail at this juncture.

Regarding the representation issue, my fundamental claim is for the superiority of procedural mechanisms—such as elections—for establishing leadership in a normally functioning liberal polity. This claim rests on a dual foundation: (1) normative commitment to democratic participation and rational discourse as the means of making political decisions; and (2) a contention that representation based on allegations of organicism does not, except under extraordinary conditions of popular mobilization, satisfy the requirements of those norms, certainly not among a constituency as large, diffuse, and differentiated as black Americans. Electoral representation requires public validation at regular intervals; organic representation, on the other hand, sidesteps the problem of validation by assuming automatically that the interests of representatives and constituents are identical. This hypothetical identity can be tested only by the "people in motion," and, because mass activism is not an ordinary state of affairs in a liberal polity, opportunities for popular validation can occur only in epic circumstances, which are rare by definition. Electorally based leadership is thus in principle generally more accountable than organically based leadership. Electoral legitimations are also in principle generally preferable to organic ones in relation to discursive and participatory values. The growth of elected officialdom, therefore, *potentially* exerts a democratizing influence on leadership selection and agenda formation in the black community.

This view, it should be noted, does not of itself constitute an argument for the relative propriety of the "really existing" stratum of black elected officials. Recognition that elaboration of an electoral politics opens democratic possibilities in the black community is not tantamount to exaltation of contemporary politicians. On the contrary, I have indicated that current protest and elective elites are equally disposed to define their relationship to their black constituents in organic terms. They are equally averse to public debate and equally impatient with public scrutiny. In general, black elected officials do not appear less indifferent than protest spokespersons toward actualizing democratic values in the black community; nor do they seem any more capable of generating commanding political vision. Yet mediocre or unsatisfactory leadership that must stand for recertification before an electorate can be chastened or replaced far more easily than can leadership that does not have to meet that test. Even though electoral legitimations do not necessarily alter the quality of representation in the here-and-now, they at least carry a built-in, unambiguous, and accessible mechanism for repudiation of the inadequate or undesirable. Therefore, even in the present situation—in which elective and organic leadership does not differ greatly with regard to political style or program—electoral representation is nonetheless preferable to the alternatives.

Establishment of the democratic superiority of electoral representation does not exhaust the issue, however. Efficacy is distinct from consonance with democratic interests as a criterion for comparison. Because they control more immediately consequential political resources, elected officials may be more likely than their protest counterparts to succeed in realizing the policy agendas they set for themselves. The catch, of course, is that for several good and not so good reasons—most having to do with being reelected—those agendas are not likely to be especially visionary. Furthermore, because elected officials represent territorial jurisdictions that include a variety of constituencies, their agendas must account explicitly for interests outside the black population. In addition to the obligation to represent the various local interests, elected officials also must accommodate (or at least acknowledge) the strategic concerns of the national and state party structures to which they are linked—a situation no different from any other officeholders attempting to formulate and realize agendas through the regular processes of the American political system. Protest politicians are not similarly encumbered by mandated requirements to attend to interests outside the black community; nor are they similarly disciplined by the imperative to tend first to a specific territorial jurisdiction. It would appear, therefore, that although elected officials may be better at "getting things done," protest spokespersons may be more reliable at articulating authentically racial interests.

The problem with that view, however, is that protest politicians actually may be more dependent on external linkages than elected officials are. Elected officials' political authority flows directly from national and state constitutions and municipal charters. Protest politicians, except in unusual instances that allow for popular acclamation (for example, the civil rights movement), derive their authority indirectly through recognition by public officials, private elites, and public opinion media. Certainly elected officials also are responsive to the interests of those centers of power outside the black community. A major difference, though, is leverage; in bargaining with white elite interests, elected officials are strengthened both by possession of statutory public authority and by demonstrated capacity to accumulate black votes, while protest politicians most often can only importune and postulate their organic representation of a hypothetical black constituency. Moreover, elected officials—at least after their initial elections—are more likely to depend only secondarily on external, nongovernmental financial support (for campaign funds, special projects, and graft). Protest politicians rely on external funding sources for primary needs, including their daily subsistence.

The foregoing considerations suggest that, to the extent that the two groups claim functional responsibility for articulating political agendas on behalf of the general black community and realizing them through regular political processes, elected officials both have a more plausible, more legitimate basis for asserting popular mandate and are more efficacious than their organic/protest counterparts. Elective representation is superior with regard to political capacity and potential for realizing democratic values when the following conditions pertain:

1. Both elective officials and protest spokespersons opt for the role of articulating collective racial interests;

2. both are committed to operating within the strategic parameters defined by the "rules of the game" of growth politics (see chapter 5), particularly the framework of elite brokerage for stipulated interest groups;

3. both concentrate on incremental programs and policy objectives that can be attained without serious disruption of existing patterns of distribution and therefore through the normal process of consensual—or at least nonconfrontational—negotiation with governmental and other significant elites; and

4. no intersubjectively verifiable participatory alternative exists to election to public office as a basis upon which to validate claims to racial group representation.

These conditions have prevailed from the early 1970s into the mid-1980s, and as long as they persist the prognosis for organic leadership is redundancy and eventual obsolescence. Extrapolation from the present situation, therefore, yields a three-part scenario for organic/protest leadership.

First of all, things most likely will remain pretty much as they are. Because of the apparent absence of pressures for change, the tension between competing claims to racial leadership by organic/protest and elective elites probably will remain latent for the most part, perhaps with an occasional eruption into overt conflict, as happened with the Jackson campaign. At the same time, specialized racial interest research or advocacy groups, such as Trans Africa or the Joint Center for Political Studies, gradually may become more visible. As Martin Kilson and Robert Smith have noted, those groups tend to accept the priority of elective officials as a precondition for their activities. They thus forfeit any claim to carry political proxies for the black community; instead, their focus tends to be more technical and directed toward specific interest groups. Their increasing prominence, therefore, would represent a further erosion of the status of organic/protest leadership.

Among the latter, the style of race relations engineering that Earl Picard has identified well may continue to proliferate, as he suggests. For one thing, the aura of professionalism and expertise that surrounds this style of racial brokerage is attractive ideologically to upper-strata black protest functionaries, who need a basis for legitimation that warrants claims to high status and does not require mass mobilization. In that sense race relations engineering is in part simply another trip down a road in American culture already traversed by medicine, social work, industrial relations, the various fiefdoms in the social sciences, and cosmetology. Moreover, direct negotiation of affirmative action "covenants" with private corporate elites is desirable instrumentally because (a) it does not require intermediation of often cumbersome and delicate state or other public processes; (b) it allows, by proceeding within the private sector logic of profitability, for unrestrained concentration on an agenda tailored specifically and exclusively to advance the position of upper-income, upwardly mobile blacks; and (c) it is an appropriate concession to the current American *realpolitik* of retrenchment, at least from the standpoint of the antipolitical, accommodationist pragmatism that has organized the worldview of much of the black petit bourgeoisie since Booker T. Washington. A turn to this engineering style also constitutes a de facto concession of political leadership to elective officials—except insofar as the only bargaining chip held by race relations engineers is the threat of boycott or other mass disruption. (That exception, however, reveals a major limitation of this "corporate interventionist" strategy; its operative components are essentially contradictory. The antipolitical focus on private negotiation of privately determined agendas cannot be reconciled with the eminently political threat of agitation of public discontent. That contradiction strongly suggests that this strategy can be applied only—as it has been so far—to corporations that already are concerned, for whatever reasons, with race relations. Any recalcitrant firm simply would call what must be an empty bluff.)

On the other hand, the mystique of the Jackson campaign and the persistence of its Rainbow myth indicate that many observers hold to a different scenario for the future of organic/protest leadership among Afro-Americans. In that scenario protest politics might once again (as it did from the late 1950s to the early 1970s) become associated with grass-roots organization and popular activism. That view is nurtured by the fact that the gains attainable through regular pluralist processes leave much to be desired for much of the black population. Ronald Walters and others in fact have proposed (see chapter 1) a division of labor between protest and elective elites such that the former would operate outside or on the margins of the formal political system, exerting pressure to make the system more responsive to the programs of black officials. A grass-roots, activist movement that functioned in that way would pose a credible alternative to electoral legitimations and would overcome the protest style's apparent superfluity. However, although this scenario sounds reasonable enough on its face, it glosses certain difficulties that appear overwhelming under presently foreseeable circumstances.

One is that it is contingent on protest elites' generating the kind of critical political vision and program that would be required to build, not to mention sustain, a popular political movement; yet not only have they shown themselves bereft of critical political ideas, but their bankruptcy in that department is much of the basis for their loss of status relative to elected officials in the first place. Another difficulty is related to this problem of political vision. As I have argued in chapter 5 and elsewhere, ever since the civil rights/black power–era, black political elites of both types have defined agendas that have been geared to the narrow interests of the comparatively advantaged strata within the Afro-American population. There is little reason to expect that protest elites will disengage from the class program—which after all serves themselves and their primary reference groups—that they have been so instrumental in crafting. The prospects for creating a popular movement on the basis of an exclusively petit bourgeois class agenda are exceeding slim, as the failure to generate widespread black activism around the Bakke case showed.

Finally, this scenario's credibility is built on a seriously flawed analogy with the civil rights movement. The mass movement in the South was triggered by local protest elites who were alienated from regular political processes. (Demonstration of this point is the real contribution of Aldon Morris's study of southern activism between 1953 and 1963, despite his quite different interpretation of his findings.) That local protest leadership was in some ways alienated also from national protest elites, particularly in the NAACP. One of the most significant transformations wrought by the success of civil rights activism has been the structural integration of local black elites into regular processes on both national and local levels. As a result, local protest spokespersons (functionaries in racial advocacy organizations, vocal clergy, and the like) have little need or desire to mobilize popular political insurgency, if only because their successful integration entails defining the limits of political activism as coterminous with the range of objectives attainable through regular processes.

The only possible source for origination of grass-roots activism in this context, barring a catastrophic disruption of the status of entrenched black elites (for example, complete and emphatic rejection by both Democratic and Republican parties), is the development of some as yet unknowable "third force" in the black community. At this point, however, no clues exist as to how and from what sector such a force might be constituted. Therefore, although the possible development of some such force must be kept alive as an emancipatory principle, that possibility cannot realistically inform practice in the foreseeable future.

How, then, can emancipatory interests be advanced among Afro-Americans in this situation? Any specific proposals must be directed toward two pressing objectives: (1) participation in construction of a political counteroffensive in the struggle against the retrenchment associated with Reaganism; and (2) cultivation of a sphere of critical, democratic discourse about politics within the black community. These two projects clearly are distinct. The first mainly concerns the relation of blacks to other status groups in the polity; the second focuses on processes of interest articulation among black Americans as a discrete, yet internally differentiated, element of the citizenry. However, the two projects are compatible. They can, perhaps even must, proceed simultaneously. The prevailing frameworks for discussing and doing politics in the black community are incapable of generating the kind of vision required for a credible counteroffensive against the rightist onslaught. (As I have shown, those frameworks are deeply implicated in the atrophy of a critical politics among blacks in the post–civil rights era.) At the same time, the revanchist ideology of the right threatens to alter the orientation of American politics in ways that would expel blacks from the national policy consensus. What follows are rudimentary proposals of modest strategies for meeting those two critical objectives.

With regard to the external objective, the urgency of the present situation and the absence of other significant organizational arenas in any way open to social democratic objectives combine to decree that the Democratic party (notwithstanding the occasional local exception) is the principal and most important terrain for concerted black political action. The Republican party is dominated by two tendencies that render it unthinkable as a medium for politics sensitive to values of equality and human rights. One, in a style that hints at charges of a black *Kulturschande,* openly panders to such racist sentiments as exist in the white electorate, deploying demagoguery about "crime," "welfare fraud," or "traditional values" in a scarcely veiled assault on black-identified legislation and programs as such; the other, while opposing gratuitous racism and advocating recruitment/creation of a black rightwing presence in the party, defines itself—no less than does the first—by an economic and fiscal agenda that concentrates the costs of growth on large, already disadvantaged sectors of the minority population. At this point, no meaningful space exists in the GOP that is not mortgaged to a program of economic and social reaction.

Frustration over the lack of systemic alternatives has contributed to expressions of concern that the Democrats "take blacks for granted" and to calls for formation of an independent black party or some other course that would remove blacks from the mainline debate over redirection of public policy. Two practicalities make any such strategy both wrongheaded and dangerous under present conditions. First, no popular base currently exists within the black community for wide-scale political organization independent of the Democratic party. Most politically attentive blacks (including public officials) identify as Democrats, and there is scant indication that that will change appreciably in the near future. Without the weight of popular support, an independent initiative would be unable to force its terms of discourse onto public debate and would be doomed to act out an irrelevant politics of wish-fulfillment.

Second, a central element in the right's agenda is reformulation of the character of American political discourse not only to strip the state of its mandate to reduce inequality but also to extirpate the idea of any such mandate from the political culture. (This ideological-cultural offensive is exemplified clearly in the publications of Charles Murray, Midge Decter, George Gilder, and others who are more—or some-

times less—subtle about their intent.) Already, the proliferation of much of what is known as "neoliberalism" within
Democratic ranks reflects the progress of that agenda (for example, specious allegations made that the party has lost ground
because of its capture by minorities and other "special interests"). In this environment black concession of the right to
struggle over the party's future would be tantamount to acquiescence in the program of those forces that would drive
blacks to the margins of the polity. Considering the vicious-
ness lurking in the Reaganite attempt to stigmatize government action on behalf of minorities as the source of American
decline, the implications of such acquiescence could be grave.

The Democratic party is important not only as a forum but
also as a source of allegiances outside the black community.
The labor movement, which has been wedded to the party for
many of the same reasons as have Afro-Americans, remains
the most powerful and most consistent proponent of even a
mildly social democratic policy orientation in mainstream
American politics. (It is worthwhile to recall that current proclamations by rightists of labor's death as a political force are
prescriptive in design as well as descriptive.) The AFL-CIO's
1984 platform proposals showed that organized labor certainly is amenable to negotiating a new political agenda that
counters the right's initiative and preserves the principle of
governmental commitment to social justice. In addition to labor, the Democratic party is the main vehicle of political action for Jews—whose "defection" to the Republicans turned
out to be so much right-wing wishful thinking—feminists, other
minorities, and civil libertarians, and these groups provide a
solid base within which to generate the needed critical opposition to antiegalitarian tendencies both inside the party and
without.

Although tensions exist within and among those different
groups, each has an independent interest in defeat of the right;
the party—and the struggle for its future—can serve as the

concrete political context for formation of an effective coalition against retrenchment. Moreover, the strategic and programmatic efforts required to construct such a coalition might indeed set in motion a social democratic alliance that could eventually expand or transcend the corporate growth–bound horizons that until now have circumscribed Democratic vision. Prospects for transforming the party into a rigorously social-democratic entity are, of course, remote; however, at this moment in American history it is a vital organizational agency for any broad-scale emancipatory initiative in practical politics, including those that emanate from the black community.

The situation differs somewhat, though not completely, for the other pressing project confronting a critical black politics. As I have argued throughout this book, development of electoral legitimations within the black community does not automatically make substantive representation any more democratic. The long-standing antiparticipatory style of organic spokesmen has been reproduced among elective leadership, and as a result the entrenched elites have been able with impunity to identify collective racial interest with an exceedingly narrow class agenda. The main focus for practical political acitvity within the black community in this context must be breaking down the illusion of a single racial opinion. For this internal objective, political will and courage are more important than party apparatus.

A first step must be to cultivate a spirit of civic liberalism in Afro-American politics. Dissent must be dissociated from the stigma of race treason, and principles of rational political argument and open participation must be brought to bear on the relation between representatives and those represented. The cause of civic liberalism can be advanced only by practicing it. This entails an obligation for all citizens, especially intellectuals (who after all supposedly engage in such behavior for their living), to maintain close, public, critical scrutiny of

claims made by political elites and to demand public account-
ing for and judgment of their actions. A systematic attack must
be launched on the prevailing pattern in which justification of
elite behavior occurs autocratically, by reference to status and
authority of person; insistence on public justification by means
of rational-discursive principles is a sine qua non of democratic community.

Civil liberalism also requires encouragement of dissent and
debate over as wide a range of issues and perspectives as possible. Letting a "hundred flowers bloom, hundred schools of
thought contend" would constitute a significant advance for
democratic interests in black political life. Ironically, by
pressing an unpopular position—even a fundamentally antidemocratic and antiegalitarian one—the "new black con-
servatism" may assist the cause of democracy among Afro-
Americans. While it is most unlikely that the black neocon-
servatives ever will develop a sizeable constituency in the black
community, their persistence may prod their adversaries to
clarify their own stances, to the benefit of the general quality
of black political discourse. Moreover, the shrillness with which
conservatives promulgate their critiques of established leadership may, even without popularizing their world view, fuel
expansion of the discursive realm simply by example.

If it is to be at all purposive, however, civic liberalism needs
a clear normative foundation, and it is here that the most ex-
citing possibilities exist for joining the rational-discursive and
participatory components of the democratic project in the black
community. Opening the sphere of public debate must entail
stimulating widespread popular discussion of the proper character of political community and goals of politics in general
as well as the intentional orientation and proper objectives of
black political activity. The conventions undergirding elite
political practice as a rule have been far removed from the
purview of the black citizenry, and that has had much to do
with the ease with which collective aspirations have been

subsumed into elite agendas. The effort to popularize normative discourse is a practical step toward democratizing processes of agenda formation in the black community at the same time that it has more abstract implications for enhancing rational civic culture.

The proposals that I have made here are, as I promised, very modest and rudimentary. They are modest in the sense that they seek to respond only to the possibilities immediately available in the present (mainstream) political situation, with no greater expectations. They are rudimentary in that they are virtually devoid of mechanical detail. However, their lack of range and development is intentional. Speculation concerning the ultimate content of a new Democratic agenda is fatuous at this point; a substantive political program can arise only from coalitional activity within the party. Similarly, the programmatic outcomes of the democratization of black political discourse lie too far down the road to be envisaged. Thus the underdeveloped character of the proposals expresses the extent to which emancipatory interests are constrained in the political context of the mid-1980s. To that extent also these proposals, and the analysis from which they derive, remind us that discussion of political strategy, of whatever variety, always must take the "really existing" political situation—no matter how unpalatable—as a point of departure. Perhaps that is their radical implication.

Notes

Chapter 1

1. The ritualistic factor is disguised through an emphasis on Jackson as the "first" black presidential candidate. In fact, Shirley Chisholm ran in Democratic primaries in 1972; various Communist party and SWP candidates have been black; Eldridge Cleaver ran on the Peace and Freedom ticket and Dick Gregory as an Independent 1968, and even Clennon King, the Baptist minister and former mental patient who received media attention for attempting to integrate Jimmy Carter's church in 1976, had run as an Independent in 1960. Presumably, Jackson's hold on originality is secured by the qualifier "serious." Yet what are the criteria of seriousness? Jackson supporters acknowledged from the onset that he had no chance to win the nomination, and Cleaver, Chisholm, King, and the others can make equal claim to "moral victory," whatever that is in an electoral context that reduces ineluctably to a zero-sum relation of winners and losers.

2. See, for example, Martin Schram and Dan Balz, "Jackson's Run Poses Dilemma for Black Leaders," *Washington Post* (November 27, 1983).

3. Ronald Walters, "The Black Politician: Fulfilling the Legacy of Black Power," *Current History* 67 (November 1974): 200 ff.

4. Robert Smith, "Black Power and the Transformation from Protest to Politics," *Political Science Quarterly* 96 (Fall 1981): 431–43.

5. Martin Kilson, "The New Black Political Class," in Joseph Washington, ed., *Dilemmas of the Black Middle Class* (Philadelphia, 1980), 81–100.

6. I have examined the logic of the integration of black extrasystemic political activity in the 1960s in "Black Particularity Reconsidered," *Telos* (Spring 1979): 71–93, and in revised and updated form in "The 'Black Revolution' and the Reconstruction of Domination," in Adolph Reed, Jr., ed., *Race, Politics and Culture: Critical Essays on the Radicalism of the 1960s* (Westport: Greenwood Press, forthcoming 1986). Also see my introduction to that volume for a critique of recent functionalist social scientific reconstructions of protest activity.

7. Alex Willingham discusses theoretical and practical contours of this tension in "Ideology and Politics: Their Status in Afro-American Social Theory," in Reed, forthcoming.

8. A flavor of the role of this developing basis for conflict in relation to the 1983 march can be seen in Eric Pianin, "The March and the Dream; The Impact: New Laws and Realities, D.C.: From Protest to Power," *Washington Post* (August 27, 1983).

9. Sheila Rule, "Black Caucus in Capital Works to Develop Communal Leadership," *New York Times* (September 30, 1981).

10. Ibid.

11. Roger Wilkins, "Black Leaders and Needs," *New York Times* (September 28, 1981).

12. Martin Kilson, "Political Change in the Negro Ghetto, 1900–1940s," in Nathan I. Higgins, Martin Kilson, and Daniel M. Fox, eds., *Key Issues in the Afro-American Experience*, 2 vols. (New York, 1971), 2: 167–92. Kilson traces this modernizing tendency's development in relation to a "clientage" model that operated prior to the advent of widespread black electoral participation.

13. Rule, "Black Caucus," and Wilkins, "Black Leaders."

14. Rule, "Black Caucus."

15. Ronald Walters, "The Challenge of Black Leadership: An Analysis of the Problem of Strategy Shift," *Urban League Review* 5 (Summer 1980). Walters, a political scientist and for years an advocate of service to black politicians, became Jackson's chief policy advisor. See Ronald Smothers, "Jackson Advisers Are Diverse Group," *New York Times* (March 25, 1984).

16. Reed, "Black Particularity," and "The 'Black Revolution.' " Earl Picard examines this development through analysis of a focal shift by extragovernmental black elites over the 1970s and early 1980s from an emphasis on "state interventionist" to direct "corporate interventionist" strategies to press black claims. Picard argues convincingly that this shift

institutionally influences black interest articulation processes, reflecting and reinforcing the uncoupling of an exclusively elite agenda. This argument is developed in "The New Black Economic Development Strategy," *Telos* (Summer 1984): 53–64. Picard's analysis implies a perspective on the likely form that a successful intraelite division of labor would take. Public officials could claim "state intervention" strategy as their proper sphere, ceding responsibility for "corporate interventionist" lobbying to a protest elite reconstituted professionally as civil rights engineers. The fact that Picard singles out Jesse Jackson's Operation PUSH—with its corporate boycott program—as a central force in this strategic shift indicates, however, that such a rational allocation of roles has hardly yet occurred.

17. Robert A. Jordan, "New Battles for Chicago Mayor," *Boston Globe* (February 7, 1984).

18. Robert C. Smith and Joseph P. McCormick II, "The Challenge of a Black Presidential Candidacy," *New Directions* (April 1984): 42.

19. Roger Wilkins, "Why Blacks May Not Follow in Droves behind White Democrats," *Washington Post National Weekly Edition* (August 6, 1984), 24.

Chapter 2

1. Barbara Reynolds, *Jesse Jackson: The Man, the Movement, the Myth* (Chicago, 1975), 238. Reynolds records that Jackson began floating the idea of a black presidential candidacy—presumably his own—as early as 1972.

2. Andrew Kopkind, "Black Power in the Age of Jackson," *The Nation* (November 26, 1983), and Barry Commoner, "Jackson's Historic Campaign," *New York Times* (July 10, 1984).

3. This response was recorded mainly in informal conversations with Jackson supporters, several of whom went so far as to indict AFL-CIO duplicity as a principal cause of such black Mondale voting as there was.

4. See, for example, "Jackson's Campaign: A Diverse Appeal," *Washington Post* (April 29, 1984). Andrew Young's adviser, Stoney Cooks, linked the Jackson insurgency to a "new protest for black aspiring classes," identifying Jackson's main public as "a new and excited group . . . who want to be part of the presidential process and who haven't been involved in it before . . . people who are middle-class and better. People who, when Jesse Jackson's PUSH convention came to Atlanta, could afford to stay in the first-class hotels" (Schram and Balz, "Jackson's Run"). James Turner, a Cornell professor and Jackson adviser, in discussing the postconvention bugbear of black "enthusiasm," indicated that it was the "new poeple, the

young professionals, who were willing to go out and beat the bushes for Jesse'' (quoted in Wilkins, ''Why Blacks May Not Follow'').

5. David E. Rosenbaum, ''Black Democrats in the Poll Prefer Mondale to Jackson as Nominee,'' *New York Times* (July 10, 1984). A *Newsweek* poll two months earlier found that 51 percent of black Democrats favored Mondale as a candidate, compared to 38 percent for Jackson. Moreover, only 29 percent of black respondents listed Jackson as their second choice, and only 11 percent felt that Jackson ''represents black Americans better than any one person'' (*Newsweek* [May 7, 1984]: 42).

6. Ibid.

7. In this regard a likely scenario, suggested by individuals close to local politics in various black communities, shows black Democrats going through the motions of Jackson support—both for affective reasons and because Jackson's status had come to define the terrain of black political discourse—yet maintaining their ultimate commitment to Mondale. See, for example, John Lewis's comments quoted in Rosenbaum, ''Black Democrats.''

8. Of the 695,000 black voters added to southern rolls between 1980 and 1984, 647,000 registered after 1982. The 1982–84 figures are taken from Voter Education Project, ''Black Voter Registration in the South, 1940–1982,'' mimeo, 1984.

9. Between 1970 and 1974 the rate of increase was 14.9 percent. Overall, an increase of 26.7 percent occurred in the 1970s (ibid). The reduction in the rate of increase in the 1976–80 period may reflect that registration had reached a ''natural'' threshold.

10. Furthermore, Arkansas, with a recorded rate of increase of 19 percent, had had a major gubernatorial race against a Republican incumbent in 1982; the same situation occurred in Texas (16 percent increase). Louisiana (15 percent increase) had highly charged state races anchored by opposition to a Republican gubernatorial incumbent in 1983, and in Georgia (15 percent increase)—like North Carolina—regular Democrats initiated a systematic registration drive from the governor's office aimed largely at the black community in anticipation of Republican challenges. When these states are bracketed along with the top three, the rate of increase in the rest of the region is slightly over 7 percent. See Thomas E. Cavanagh and Lorn S. Foster, ''Jesse Jackson's Campaign: The Primaries and Caucuses,'' *Joint Center for Political Studies, Election '84: Report No. 2* (Washington, D.C., 1984).

11. I am grateful to Brian Sherman, research director of the Voter Education Project, for noting this caveat.

12. Among these are several gathered under the rubric of the National

Coalition for Black Voter Participation and its "Operation Big Vote" begun in 1982. Included in this coalition are the NAACP, AFL-CIO, Democratic National Committee, National Urban League, A. Philip Randolph Institute, Voter Education Project, Operation PUSH, and the Joint Center for Political Studies, as well as other, more local or regional groups. Many of these efforts are discussed in Joel Rogers, "The Politics of Voter Registration," *The Nation* (July 21–28, 1984), and Joseph Clark, "The American Blacks: A Passion for Politics," *Dissent* (Summer 1984): 261–64.

13. From October 1983 through April 1984, the Jesse Jackson for President Campaign Committee contained no line item related to voter registration in its budget (Cavanagh and Foster, 27). Although the campaign presumably conducted registration efforts indirectly through Operation PUSH, this could not have entailed much more than assisting in the ongoing efforts of other groups.

14. Ibid., 17. That some of this increase may reflect opposition to Reagan independent of Jackson's candidacy is indicated by the fact that national black voter turnout in 1982 elections already was up 15.6 percent from 1978 levels (see Rogers, 48). The 1984 turnout findings, moreover, may suggest a further limitation on Jackson's purported registration effect. In three reporting states the black turnout included 11 percent first-time voters and in another 9 percent. In the remaining five states first-time voters hovered around 4–5 percent of the total black turnout (Cavanagh and Foster, 17).

15. "Two Blacks Are Defeated Despite Jackson's Drive," *Wall Street Journal* (May 10, 1984).

16. Spaulding's and Hall's figures were obtained from the Joint Center for Political Studies. Jackson's were taken from *Congressional Quarterly* (May 12, 1984), 1118–20.

17. John Herbers, "Alabama Voting: Some Gains for Blacks," *New York Times* (July 12, 1984).

18. Ronald Smothers, "Beyond the Jackson Bid: Some Gains for Blacks," *New York Times* (July 1, 1984).

19. Southern Regional Council, *An Analysis of Voting Patterns in Alabama and Georgia: The Presidential Primary Election of March 13, 1984* (Atlanta, 1984).

20. Dudley Clendinen, "Computer-Aided Black Network Won Louisiana for Jackson," *New York Times* (May 7, 1984). The Louisiana case was marred by controversy. The governor, after losing a court battle to cancel the primary, publicly urged voters to boycott it.

21. Robert A. Jordan, "White Backlash Feared in Election," *Boston Globe* (May 20, 1984).

22. Cavanagh and Foster, 17. Despite a black increase of 14 percent, Georgia as a whole experienced a 34 percent decrease in voting from 1980.

23. Thomas B. Edsall, "Southern Blacks Set Voting Record; Northern White Rate Sagged," *Washington Post* (March 15, 1984).

24. Ellen Hume, "GOP Views Jackson as a Plus," *Wall Street Journal* (July 11, 1984). See also "Who's Registering?" *Washington Post* (September 11, 1984), and Thomas B. Edsall, "GOP Has Standoff in Registration," *Washington Post* (September 16, 1984).

25. See, for example, Garry Wills, "Jesse Jackson over the Rainbow," *Gentlemen's Quarterly* (February 1984): 144 f. William Bradford Reynolds even joined Jackson to sing "We Shall Overcome" at a Mississippi voter registration rally (Curtis Wilkie, "Jackson Preaches Voting Power," *Boston Globe* [July 10, 1983]).

26. Hume, "GOP Views Jackson." This article also suggests that the registration drives conducted by Falwell's Moral Majority have drawn support from publicity attending Jackson's effort. In Jesse Helm's close race for reelection to his senate seat from North Carolina the Moral Majority led a church-based registration drive that helped to add over 539,000 white voters to the rolls (26 percent increase). Black registration in the senate increased by 247,000 (61 percent). Even though the black rate of increase is more impressive, the absolute white increase swamps it (William E. Schmidt, "Caustic North Carolina Senate Race Is Ending Up a Dead Heat," *New York Times* [November 4, 1984]).

27. Cavanagh and Foster, 14.

28. James R. Dickenson, "Jackson Seen Aiding, Hurting Ticket," *Washington Post* (August 31, 1984). In the South the disparity was wider: 19 percent less likely, 8 percent more likely.

29. Ronald Smothers, "Jackson Said to Ponder Race for Senate in South Carolina," *New York Times* (July 15, 1984). Jackson dropped this plan within two weeks.

30. This disposition was especially striking in the races against Addabo and Rodino. See Michael Norman, "Behind the Challenge to an 18-Term Congressman," *New York Times* (May 31, 1984), and Robert W. Merry, "Black Challenger in Queens: New Politics Threatens Addabo," *Wall Street Journal* (September 10, 1984).

31. Bill Peterson and Milton Coleman, "Southern Black Vote Buoys Jackson Bid," *Washington Post* (March 14, 1984).

32. Gerald M. Boyd, "Jackson Sees a Victory amid Black Frustration," *New York Times* (July 20, 1984).

33. Jordan, "New Battles for Chicago Mayor."

34. William E. Schmidt, "A Rival for Georgia Seat Puts Bond on the Stump," *New York Times* (August 14, 1984).

35. Ronald Smothers, "Disputes among Blacks Threaten Efforts by Democrats in the South," *New York Times* (August 28, 1984).

36. Thomas E. Cavanagh and Denise Stockton, *Black Elected Officials and Their Constituencies* (Washington, D.C., 1983), 9.

37. Ibid., 10.

38. Ibid., 13.

39. The Northeast and North Central regions account for 34 percent of black officialdom, the West only 6 percent (ibid., 6).

40. Ibid., 5.

Chapter 3

1. I have examined this phenomenon as an element of the shared conventional understanding that structured the conflict between DuBois and Washington. On this plane, a major dynamic operative in that conflict was Washington's monopoly over access to legitimacy among white elites. See Adolph Reed, Jr., "W. E. B. DuBois: A Perspective on the Bases of His Political Thought," *Political Theory* 13 (August 1985): 431–56.

2. Although this organicism also undergrids nationalist and other types of extrasystemic activism, those are exempted from this analysis. My concern here is with only those black populist expressions that arise within the fundamentally intrasystemic protest orientation.

3. James M. Perry, "Jackson Race Has Familiar Ring," *Wall Street Journal* (May 10, 1984), and Paul Berman, "Jackson and the Left: The Other Side of the Rainbow," *The Nation* (April 7, 1984): 407–08.

4. The Reaganite Right acknowledges this phenomenon with almost embarrassing frankness by expressing a desire to create its own black leadership. See William Raspberry, "Inventing Black Leaders," *Washington Post* (December 21, 1983).

5. Thomas Oliphant, "Jesse Jackson: He's Generating Interest despite Campaign's Problems," *Boston Globe* (December 15, 1983).

6. "Jesse Jackson Speaks: 'I Could Have Won,' " *Ebony* (August 1984): 168.

7. Howell Raines, "Parties Study Jackson Role in Convention," *New York Times* (April 8, 1984).

8. See, for example, Ellen Hume, "Jackson Backers Look to Him to Help Blacks Get 'Our Fair Share,' " *Wall Street Journal* (June 1, 1984). The *Journal*'s informal survey of black Democrats in Newark revealed a primary interest in "bread and butter" issues, none of which surfaced in Jackson's convention agenda.

9. Peterson and Coleman, "Southern Black Vote."

10. From the transcript of the Corporation for Public Broadcasting's *Frontline* broadcast on April 2, 1984. The transcript citation is *Frontline* no. 208, "The Struggle for Birmingham," 20.

11. See, for example, Fay S. Joyce, "Jackson Citing 'My Integrity,' Upholds His Ties to Farrakhan," *New York Times* (May 6, 1984); E.R. Shipp, "Black Journalists Debate Reporter's Use of Jackson Remark," *New York Times* (August 17, 1984); E.R. Shipp, "Black Reporters Sum Up Disputes," *New York Times* (August 20, 1984); and Milton Coleman, "18 Words, Seven Weeks Later," *Washington Post* (April 8, 1984).

12. Less than a week later my adolescent son, then in Atlanta, related a similar argument made by the parents of one of his friends—again well-educated, middle class people. Laetril politics knows no racial bounds!

13. Fay S. Joyce, "In Slums, Fields and a Hall of Graduates, Jackson Strives to Turn On Hope," *New York Times* (May 7, 1984).

14. "Jesse Jackson Speaks," 170. He went on to evoke images of wheelchair faithful and the "spirit of resurrection."

15. Ibid.

Chapter 4

1. Wilkie, "Jackson Preaches Voting Power."

2. James M. Perry, "Banner Day for Jesse: One-Man Band Excites Crowds," *Wall Street Journal* (February 21, 1984).

3. The pervasiveness of religious imagery in Jackson's performance is captured in Dudley Clendinen, "Nation Is a Cathedral with Jackson at Pulpit," *New York Times* (July 19, 1984).

4. Betty Anne Williams, "Jesse Jackson: President Reagan Fails 'Character Test,' " *Baton Rouge Morning Advocate* (September 30, 1984). At a Memphis rally with Geraldine Ferraro, Jackson summoned the authority of "Jesus Himself" to inveigh against Reagan (Maureen Dowd, "Ferraro-Jackson Team Rouses Memphis Rally," *New York Times* [October 4, 1984]).

5. However, clerical leadership may be more proficent at collecting funds for mobilization than in actually turning out voters. In the 1976 presidential campaign Jimmy Carter, who—as a fellow Baptist—was not awed by their homilies, insisted that a group of West Coast ministers return campaign money for which they had done no work. See Grayson Mitchell, "Carter Street Money a Problem?" and "Black Religious Groups Return Carter Cash," *Atlanta Constitution* (August 11, 1976). Also see Robert Sam Anson, "The New Hustlers," *New Times* (1977).

6. Norman, "Behind the Challenge."

7. "New Voters, Ministers among Jackson Backers," and "The Rev. Willie Wilson: Gaining Self-Sufficiency," *Washington Post* (April 29, 1984). Also see Cavanagh and Foster, 13.

8. *Frontline*, "Struggle for Birmingham," 8.

9. Kilson, "New Black Political Class," 87.

10. Floyd Hunter discusses this case in *Community Power Succession: Atlanta's Policy-Makers Revisited* (Chapel Hill, 1980), 71–72. Also see Mack H. Jones, "Black Political Powerment in Atlanta: Myth and Reality," *Annals of the American Academy of Political and Social Science* (September 1978): 90–117; Peter Ross Range, "Making It in Atlanta: Capital of Black-is-Bountiful," *New York Times Magazine* (April 7, 1974); and Frederick Allen, "The 'Black Ticket' Has Been Erased," *Atlanta Constitution* (September 25, 1978).

11. W. E. B. DuBois, *The Souls of Black Folk* (New York, 1969), 113–14.

12. See Aldon D. Morris, *The Origins of the Civil Rights Movement: Black Communities Organizing for Change* (New York, 1984). Morris's desire to read the development of the civil rights movement as a church-sponsored saga is unfortunate, moreover, because it leads him to overlook other important constitutive dynamics, certain of which he even mentions in passing. He notes, for example, that in the early boycotts on which he focuses—Baton Rouge, Montgomery, Birmingham, Tallahassee, Shreveport—the ministers who assumed leadership of the local movements all were simultaneously prominent in their NAACP chapters and that in nearly all cases church-based organizations were created to serve as "movement centers" only because the NAACP had been declared subversive and outlawed by segregationist state legislatures. Despite the fact that his own findings thus suggest that NAACP membership was probably more reliable than churchliness as a predictor of activism (there were, after all, many ministers and church members in each case who were not active), Morris persists in arguing that the clerical tail wagged the dog. Similarly, in nearly every city in which protests occurred during the period Morris considers, the institutional configuration of the black community included at least one black college. Although he lists the cities, Morris is so intent on establishing the church's role that he fails to attend to the possible significance of the presence of subcommunities clustered around institutions of higher learning as sources of activism. After all, it appears—by his own evidence—that protest movements were generated within a substantially greater proportion of the cities with black colleges than within the cities with developed church-based social infrastructures.

13. Martin Luther King, Jr., *Stride Toward Freedom* (New York, 1958), 34–36.

14. Martin Luther King, Jr., *Strength to Love* (Glasgow, 1969), 62–63.

15. E. Franklin Frazier, *The Negro Church in America* (New York, 1964), 48.

16. Ibid., 49.

17. Charles S. Johnson, *Growing Up in the Black Belt: Negro Youth in the Rural South* (New York, 1941), 135. In locating the church within the "system of separate social institutions [that] retarded the development of the Negro," Johnson observed that often "religious doctrines appropriated [from whites] were in conflict with pragmatic social values" (136).

18. Ibid., 169.

19. Johnson suggests that the "indifference of the Negro church to current social issues . . . lent indirect but vital support to the race patterns of the early post-slavery period" (*Growing Up,* 136).

20. John Dollard, *Caste and Class in a Southern Town* (rpt., Garden City, 1957), 248. Schools, he noted, were not similarly welcomed.

21. Frazier, *Negro Church,* 51.

22. Ibid.

23. Allison Davis, Burleigh B. Gardner, and Mary R. Gardner, *Deep South,* abridged edition (Chicago, 1941), 246. Predictably, the planters also benefited financially from this arrangement.

24. Ibid., 247.

25. Ibid., 246.

26. Frazier, *Negro Church,* 54–57.

27. Ibid., 56.

28. St. Clair Drake and Horace Cayton, *Black Metropolis: A Study of Negro Life in a Northern City,* 2 vols. (New York, 1945), 2: 418–20, 640–53.

29. Gunnar Myrdal, *An American Dilemma: The Negro Problem and Modern Democracy,* 2 vols. (New York, 1944), 2: 876.

30. Ibid., 877.

31. Ralph J. Bunche, *The Political Status of the Negro in the Age of FDR* (Chicago, 1973), 576. Gosnell, however, found in Chicago that black churchgoers "do not ordinarily look to their ministers for the leadership that unites all the elements of a party organization" and that the "political importance of the Negro clergy is not as great in Chicago today as it was in the South during [Reconstruction]" (Harold Gosnell, *Negro Politicans: The Rise of Negro Politics in Chicago* [Chicago, 1935], 100).

32. Bunche, *Political Status,* 490. Bunche's specific reference here is

to Atlanta; however, his study found similar circumstances in Memphis and other areas of the South.

33. Ibid., 93.

34. On the eve of the Alabama primary he expatiated, "Some people said they voted for the Voting Rights Act of '65, I marched for it. They voted for the public accommodation bill of '64, I was jailed for it. They voted for open housing, I marched and talked about it. I didn't just show up to get you the right to vote" (*Frontline*, "Struggle for Birmingham," 15).

35. Doug McAdam, *Political Process and the Development of Black Insurgency, 1930–1970* (Chicago 1982), 99.

36. Ibid., 134.

37. Ibid., 133.

38. Ibid., 126. McAdam notes that the student thrust intentionally rejected church-based strategies (138).

39. Ibid., 147.

40. Ibid., 154. By comparison, the NAACP and the Congress on Racial Equality were responsible for 24 and 22 percent, respectively.

41. M. Elaine Burgess, *Negro Leadership in a Southern City* (Chapel Hill, 1960), 41.

42. Ibid., 41–42. Burgess observed, however, that the former group appeared to be growing.

43. William H. Chafe, *Civilities and Civil Rights: Greensboro, North Carolina and the Black Struggle for Freedom* (New York, 1980), 80.

44. Ibid., 20.

45. Floyd Hunter, *Community Power Structure* (Chapel Hill, 1953), 116–17. Hunter noted that this finding contraindicated "a belief abroad in the larger community that if anything is to be done through leadership in the Negro community, the ministers, the educators, and possibly the undertakers should be contacted in about that order."

46. Ibid., 118, 135.

47. Atlanta and, especially, Durham long have been understood to have unusually well-articulated black middle classes from which variegated leadership structures could develop. See, for example, E. Franklin Frazier, "Durham: Capital of the Black Middle Class," in Alain Locke, ed., *The New Negro: An Intrepretation* (New York, 1925), 333–40, and DuBois's essay, "On the Wings of Atalanta," in *The Souls of Black Folk*. In addition, a generation of political scientists and sociologists have bickered over the realiability of Hunter's reputational method.

48. Daniel C. Thompson, *The Negro Leadership Class* (Englewood Cliffs, N.J., 1963), 34.

49. Everett Carll Ladd, Jr., *Negro Political Leadership in the South* (Ithaca, 1966), 238–39.

50. Bunche, it should be recalled, adduced Atlanta as an example of the urban church's increasing concern with social affairs in the 1940s.

51. Thompson, *Negro Leadership Class,* 35. In addition, the city's black population features a bizarre mosaic of crosscutting intraracial, ethnic differentiation and cleavage.

52. Ladd, *Negro Political Leadership,* 238–39.

53. Chafe, *Civilities and Civil Rights,* 96.

54. Donald R. Matthews and James W. Prothro, *Negroes and the New Southern Politics* (New York, 1966), 233–34.

55. Burgess, *Negro Leadership,* 155.

56. Ibid., 45.

57. Ladd, *Negro Political Leadership,* 239.

58. McAdam, *Political Process,* 129.

59. Ibid.

60. Ibid.

61. Myrdal, *American Dilemma,* 877.

62. Gosnell, *Negro Politicians,* 94–95.

63. By 1984 the proportion of black respondents reporting church attendance was 42 percent (*Religion in America: 1984, Gallup Report No. 22* [March 1984], 57). Even this estimate is probably high.

64. Frazier, *Negro Church,* 90.

65. Diane Johnson, "Heart of Darkness," *New York Review of Books* (April 19, 1979), 3.

66. Frazier, 90. Recently, endorsing the mythology of clerical political leadership, Rev. Clay Evans—a Chicago Baptist pastor and former Operation PUSH board chairman—cited precisely this authoritarianism as a justification. He alleged, "The White church is not as independent as the Black church because the power of the Black church comes from the *pulpit.* The power of the White church comes from the *pews.* The Black preacher is freer to do what has to be done." Rev. William A. Jones, president of the National Black Pastors' Conference, in expressing the Jackson phenomenon's connection with this mythology, was still more direct. In his view, "The Black preacher enjoys the kind of freedom that the White preacher has never known. Hardly any White preacher can go to the pulpit and say vote for this person or that person." Evans's and Jones's comments are quoted in Thad Martin, "The Black Church: Precinct of the Black Soul," *Ebony* (August 1984): 158. This article is a paean to the church mythology.

67. Gary T. Marx, "Religion: Opiate or Inspiration of Civil Rights Militancy among Negroes?" *American Sociological Review* 32 (February 1967): 68.

68. Ibid.

69. Ibid.

70. Ibid., 69. The "not at all religious" respondents were the only category of whom a majority favored militancy.

71. Ibid.

72. Ibid., 67.

73. See West's volume, *Prophesy Deliverance! An Afro-American Revolutionary Christianity* (Philadelphia, 1982).

74. For an illustration of Jackson's politico-religious counsel, see his "Annual Address to the National Baptist Convention, 1964," in Herbert Storing, ed., *What Country Have I?* (New York, 1970), 134–43. Even at that late date Jackson declaimed against direct action. His successor as head of the seven-million-member organization, T. J. Jemison, kept the faith by warmly embracing Reagan less than two months before the 1984 election. See Francis X. Clines, "President Talks to Black Leader," *New York Times* (September 11, 1984).

75. It is noteworthy that in its response to persisting economic and political difficulties among black Americans, the Ford Foundation recently has proposed "expanding the capacity of black religious organizations and leadership to engage in new civil rights and community improvement activities," including community development demonstration projects, "rights education and documentation," and leadership development. The proposal extends also to incorporating religious institutions into ongoing Ford programs. Although the foundation's working paper floridly recycles the myth of church-based black leadership, its proposals seem designed to institutionalize a niche for the black clergy in policy processes affecting the Afro-American population. One can only wonder why Ford—which had been so instrumental in defining similar niches for the black administrative and political elite that has become entrenched since the 1960s—should now turn its attention to projecting and shoring up a different, less popularly accountable and programmatically redundant stratum in the black community. See *Civil Rights, Social Justice, and Black America: A Working Paper from the Ford Foundation* (January 1984), esp. 42–47. On Ford's role in the development of post–civil rights era black leadership infrastructure, see, for example, Geoffrey Faux and Arthur Blaustein, *The Star-Spangled Hustle* (Garden City, 1972); Robert L. Allen, *Black Awakening in Capitalist America* (Garden City, 1969); and David Horowitz and David Kolodney, "The Foundations: Charity Begins at Home," in Pamela Roby, ed., *The Poverty Establishment* (Englewood Cliffs, N.J., 1974), 43–59.

76. Karl Marx and Frederick Engels, *Collected Works* (New York, 1975), 3: 175–76.

77. Ibid., 176.

Chapter 5

1. For detailed examination of this consensual "growth politics" see Alan Wolfe, *America's Impasse: The Rise and Fall of the Politics of Growth* (Boston, 1981). John Mollenkopf reconstructs the substance of "progrowth politics" at the local level in *The Contested City* (Princeton, 1983).

2. In addition to Wolfe and Mollenkopf, Bowles et al. and Bluestone and Harrison provide thorough analyses of the decline of growth and its sources and consequences from the standpoint of political economy. See Samuel Bowles, David Gordon, and Thomas Weisskopf, *Beyond the Waste Land: A Democratic Alternative to Economic Decline* (Garden City, 1983), and Barry Bluestone and Bennett Harrison, *The Deindustrialization of America* (New York, 1982). A similar account, though from a somewhat different perspective, is found in Ira Magazinger and Robert Reich, *Minding America's Business* (New York, 1982). Different aspects of the decline of familiar styles of growth politics—including its impact on electoral alignments—are examined in the various contributions to Thomas Ferguson and Joel Rogers, eds., *The Hidden Election: Politics and Economics in the 1980 Presidential Campaign* (New York, 1981).

3. Center on Budget and Policy Priorities, *Falling Behind: A Report on How Blacks Have Fared under the Reagan Policies* (Washington, D.C., 1984), 7.

4. D. Lee Bawden and John L. Palmer, "Social Policy: Challenging the Welfare State," in John L. Palmer and Isabel V. Sawhill, eds., *The Reagan Record: An Assessment of America's Changing Domestic Priorities* (Washington, D.C., 1984), 185.

5. William P. O'Hara, *Wealth and Economic Status: A Perspective on Racial Inequality* (Washington, D.C., 1983), 25.

6. Ibid., 18.

7. Brown and Erie demonstrate the impact of approaches to racial palliation adopted since the civil rights movement on increasing economic differentiation and polarization among blacks. See Michael K. Brown and Stephen P. Erie, "Blacks and the Legacy of the Great Society: The Economic and Political Impact of Federal Social Policy," *Public Policy* 29 (Summer 1981): 299–330. Also see William J. Wilson, *The Declining Significance of Race* (Chicago, 1978), esp. 134–39.

8. Here I should note that Bowles et al. join others in arguing that, due largely to pressures from below, some redistribution did occur under the growth consensus. However, the fact that that redistribution—which the authors interpret as a breakdown of the containment strategy—helped to undermine the consensus attests to the importance of averting stimulation

of redistributive demands as a condition of the coalition's success *(Beyond the Waste Land)*, 84–97.

9. Picard discusses some of these developments in "New Black Economic Development Strategy."

10. Paul Peterson, *City Limits* (Chicago, 1981), 179.

11. Ibid., 180.

12. Piven and Cloward, for example, show that such concessions as are won by out-groups typically ensue from disruptive activity that, by raising the costs of social peace, increases new claimants' leverage and forces marginal adjustments of the distributive calculus. See Frances Fox Piven and Richard Cloward, *Poor People's Movements: Why They Succeed, How They Fail* (New York, 1977). James Button, *Black Violence: The Political Impact of the 1960s Riots* (Princeton, 1978), finds that initial federal and local governmental response to the urban uprisings was to open programmatic initiatives ostensibly aimed at alleviating the conditions of dispossession and disfranchisement that were held to be root causes. However, he notes that this mode of response stopped well short of potentially redistributive impact and quickly was discontinued after expression of opposition from established interests.

13. Compare Ronald Smothers, "Pessimism Marks Gathering of Black Lawmakers," *New York Times* (October 1, 1984); Rule, "Black Caucus"; Wilkins, "Black Leaders and Needs"; Walters, "The Challenge of Black Leadership"; Pianin, "The March and the Dream."

14. See, for example, the following: Joseph Perkins, "Are Black Leaders Listening to Black America," *Wall Street Journal* (October 16, 1984); Raspberry, "Inventing Black Leaders"; William Greider, "After Dr. King: Strong Currents of Social Change," *Washington Post* (April 2, 1978); Claude Brown, "Manchild in Harlem," *New York Times Magazine* (September 16, 1984); Thulani Davis, "Black Mayors: Can They Make the Cities Work?" *Mother Jones* (July 1984); "The Black Conservatives," *Newsweek* (March 9, 1981); Carl Rowan, "Why the Recent Black Caucus Failed," *Atlanta Constitution* (October 3, 1980); Carl Gershman, "A Matter of Class," and Kenneth Clark, "The Role of Race," *New York Times Magazine* (October 5, 1980); Lee A. Daniels, "The New Black Conservatives," *New York Times Magazine* (October 4, 1981); Brooks Jackson, "Many Blacks Show Little Urge to Vote," *Wall Street Journal* (October 3, 1980); David J. B. Blum, "Black Politicians Fear They Can't Do Much to Help Their People," *Wall Street Journal* (October 29, 1980); Thomas Sowell, "Blacker than Thou," *Washington Post* (February 13, 1981).

15. Carl Stokes, *Promises of Power: A Political Autobiography* (New York, 1973).

16. Hildred Shumake, Bond's opponent, was a thrice-unsuccessful can-

didate for public office, a member of a curious substratum of black perennial officeseekers in Atlanta who pursue political careers on the margins of credibility, devoid of reliable organizational or institutional linkages. See Schmidt, ''Rival for Georgia Seat.'' Shumake's challenge to Bond, while drawing on the latter's refusal to support Jackson, focused on the incumbent's spotty legislative record and alleged distance from constituents.

17. Jackson also drew his circle of closest advisers mainly from the cohort of functionaries in elite civil rights organizations and party politics. See Smothers, ''Jackson Advisers,'' and James Ridgeway, ''The Company He Keeps,'' *Village Voice* (July 10, 1984).

18. Picard, ''New Black Economic Development Strategy.''

19. Some of Jackson's supporters in the white Left colluded, for reasons that I shall examine in chapter 8, in mystifying this inconsistency by alleging that the demand that Jackson base his candidacy on issue positions somehow affronted the spirit of black politics. See, for example, Kopkind, ''Black Power,'' 539, 541.

20. The response of national elites to King's opposition to the Vietnam war is instructive. He was roundly denounced—even by representatives of race advocacy organizations—on the ground that foreign policy was not an appropriate area of concern for black leadership. See David L. Lewis, *King: A Critical Biography* (Baltimore, 1970), 355–59. Cession of the right to interest in broad areas of social policy as a condition of membership in the Democratic growth coalition has not been a requirement enforced only on blacks. Aronowitz finds that the AFL-CIO conceded to management's hegemony over determination of conditions and processes of production in exchange for secured material benefits (Stanley Aronowitz, *False Promises: The Shaping of American Working-Class Consciousness* [New York 1973], esp. 214–63).

21. Smith and McCormick, ''Challenge of a Black Presidential Candidacy,'' 40.

22. Ibid., 40–41.

23. Howell Raines, ''Delegates Reject 3 Bids to Change Party's Platform,'' *New York Times* (July 18, 1984). The only successful demand was the only one for which there was a discernible black constituency—strengthened commitment to affirmative action.

24. There are numerous instances in which the second primary has worked to the detriment of black and black-supported candidates. James Clyburn exemplifies a common black sentiment concerning runoffs. See his testimony before John Conyers's Subcommittee on Civil and Constitutional Rights, Committee on Judiciary, U.S. House of Representatives, Washington, D.C., June 28, 1984.

25. Key, for example, traced the origins of the runoff primary system to the one-party nature of southern politics. In his view the runoff primary is a natural product of the need to assure validation by electoral majorities in a one-party, direct primary context (V. O. Key, Jr., *Southern Politics* [New York, 1949], 417). Of course, the origins of both the direct primary and the one-party state were intimately associated with black disfranchisement. Ultimate connection, however, is not proximate causality.

26. Edward Still, "The Runoff Primary (a presentation to the Democratic National Convention Platform Committee, Birmingham, Alabama, April 24, 1984), 4. Also see Laughlin McDonald, "The Majority Vote Requirement: Its Use and Abuse in the South," *Urban Lawyer* 17 (Summer 1985): 429–39, the historically and analytically most solid of recent discussion of the dual primary issue.

27. Thomas Cavanagh, ed., *The JCPS Congressional District Fact Book* (Washington, D.C., 1984), 8–21.

28. See chapter 2, n. 5.

29. Suitts observes, somewhat cautiously, that "there appears to be white defection from the Democratic party in the South whenever blacks gain increased voting strength by whatever changes in voting procedures" (testimony of Steve Suitts before the Subcommittee on Civil and Constitutional Rights, Committee on the Judiciary, U.S. House of Representatives, June 28, 1984, p. 7).

30. Richard E. Cohen, "Many Are Skeptical about Jackson's Dual Primary Argument," *National Journal* (May 12, 1984): 923.

31. Ronald Smothers, "Jackson Pushing Democrats in South," *New York Times* (September 17, 1984); Ellen Hume, "Jackson Flair Is Welcome Bonus," *Wall Street Journal* (October 10, 1984); "Jackson Says Coalition Still Waiting for Party," *New York Times* (July 26, 1984).

32. Albert K. Karnig and Susan Welch, *Black Representation and Urban Policy* (Chicago, 1980), 149–50.

33. In 1971, 16 percent of black officeholders served in districts that were 50–69 percent black; by 1980 that complement was 21 percent of the total (Cavanagh and Stockton, *Black Elected Officials,* 20).

34. "Hosea Williams Shifts on Runoff Primaries," *New York Times* (July 13, 1984).

35. Dick Kirschten, "Democrats Weigh Party Rules Changes to Meet Jesse Jackson's Demands," *National Journal* (May 12, 1984): 922.

36. Gerald M. Boyd, "Jackson Charges Mondale Ignored Him on No. 2 Spot," *New York Times* (July 11, 1984). See also Raines, "Parties Study Jackson Role."

37. Ellen Hume and Jeanne Saddler, "Jackson Role Puzzles Demo-

crats,'' *Wall Street Journal* (July 5, 1984). Jackson's effort was distinguished by a consistent propensity to discuss his objectives in the most personalistic terms. When he vented his ire at Birmingham mayor Richard Arrington's decision to endorse Mondale in the Alabama primary, he invoked tones of personal betrayal, charging: ''I did more to make him mayor than Mondale did. I did more to open up the city than Mondale did. And what basis is there for Mondale to reap the benefits of my labor?'' (*Frontline,* ''Struggle for Birmingham,'' 7).

38. Bernard Weinraub, ''Wider Role Is Seen for Women and Blacks in Mondale Drive,'' *New York Times* (July 27, 1984); Ronald Smothers, ''Jackson's Stance Poses Questions for Campaign,'' *New York Times* (August 12, 1984).

Chapter 6

1. In mid-August, for example, Jackson complained, ''I'm not really aboard . . . I'm not part of the inner circle, for example. I'm not part of the policy-making arrangement'' (''Jackson Says Democrats Need the Black Vote,'' *New York Times* [August 17, 1984]).

2. Faye S. Joyce, ''Mondale Campaign Is Working to Win Jackson and Black Voters,'' *New York Times* (August 13, 1984); Joyce, ''Mondale Voices Irritation with Jackson's Criticisms,'' *New York Times* (August 15, 1984).

3. Even some black delegates sympathetic to Jackson cautiously expressed exasperation and perplexity at his inconsistent convention behavior. See Boyd, ''Jackson Sees a Victory.''

4. James Reston, ''Jackson's Arrogant Pride,'' *New York Times* (September 2, 1984).

5. Roger Wilkins, ''The Natural,'' *Mother Jones* (August/September 1984): 40. Wilkins went on to suggest that Jackson ''is to politics what Duke Ellington was to jazz and what Magic Johnson is to basketball.''

6. Quoted in Wilkins, ''Why Blacks May Not Follow.''

7. Ibid. Wilkins concluded: ''Enthusiasm holds the key to the black vote in November. But enthusiasm is an emotion that cannot be sustained in the company of doubts and reservations. That is why the Democrats will have to reassess their assumptions between now and Election Day and come to terms with the fact that giving respect to Jesse Jackson is symbolically giving respect to all blacks. That is the key to the level of enthusiasm that blacks bring to the Mondale-Ferraro effort.''

8. Chet Fuller, ''Don't Write off Andy Young,'' *Atlanta Constitution* (July 23, 1984).

9. Jay T. Harris, "Wave Becomes a Ripple," *Shreveport Times* (September 18, 1984).

10. Ronald Smothers, "Jackson's One Sure Legacy Is New Voters," *New York Times* (October 21, 1984).

11. Fay S. Joyce, "Leaders of Blacks Debate Conditions on Aid to Mondale," *New York Times* (August 29, 1984).

12. The AFL-CIO agenda included proposals for executive and legislative action in the following areas: public employment and training, industrial policy, international trade, monetary policy and interest rates, tax reform, labor law enforcement, unemployment insurance, social security, health care, civil rights enforcement, occupational health and safety, energy conservation, and immigration. See *The AFL-CIO Platform Proposals, Presented to the Democratic and Republican National Conventions, 1984.*

13. Lenneal J. Henderson, Jr., provides a systematic statement of the core vote thesis in "Black Politics and American Presidential Elections," in Michael Preston, Lenneal J. Henderson, Jr., and Paul Puryear, eds., *The New Black Politics: The Search for Political Power* (New York and London, 1982), 3–27. Rhetorical assertion of this claim was rife throughout the Jackson campaign. As a tribute to the self-deluding properties of ideology, this view persists despite the obvious fact that the same argument could be made regarding any of several other traditionally Democratic constituencies, all of which have combined to produce whatever electoral successes the party has enjoyed since Roosevelt. The primacy of the black vote among those constituents is a function of the vantage point of the observer; one might just as easily stand within the labor movement, the South, urban ethnic groups, or Catholics and determine that any one of them is the pivot around which the Democratic coalition revolves. The Ptolemaic perspective may be long dead in astronomy and physics, but it appears to be an "African survival" among black political analysts.

14. "Black Mayors Back Subminimum Wage for Youth," *New York Times* (May 6, 1984). Bluestone and Harrison reach the following conclusion about the enterprise zones strategy: "At best, if the enterprise-zone policy actually succeeds in cheapening labor costs, it may marginally promote the expansion of the secondary labor market. Employers who offer low-wage, low-productivity jobs and who follow authoritarian or arbitrary personnel practices are the most likely to benefit from an enterprise-zone policy. . . . Indeed, there is good reason to expect that the zones could become havens for a revival of old-fashioned sweatshops (albeit with some modern equipment like computer numerically controlled sewing machines or high-tech plastics extrusion molds)." Even the general developmental

impact of this strategy is dubious: "When it comes to promoting new small-business start-ups . . . tax breaks simply are not very helpful until a company has grown large (and successful) enough to have any profits to tax!" (*Deindustrialization,* 228).

Even then it is not clear that local tax incentives stimulate much investment that would not have occurred without them. A survey of research on the importance of local taxation policies arrives at a general finding that "relatively few firms even consider taxes in location decisions and even fewer are significantly influenced by them" (Barry M. Moriarty, *Industrial Location and Community Development* [Chapel Hill, 1980], 254). A detailed study of industrial location and investment decisions in Cincinnati and New England yields a similar conclusion. "The bulk, 40 percent to 50 percent, move within the same taxing jurisdiction or to locations in towns with similar rates. Another 25 percent move to jurisdictions with even higher property tax rates. These results are not significantly different from those that would occur by pure chance" (Robert W. Schmenner, "Industrial Location and Urban Public Management," in Arthur P. Solomon, ed., *The Prospective City* [Cambridge, Mass., 1980], 460). Schemenner finds as well that industrial revenue bonds, tax holidays, zoning changes, and other such fiscal inducements have little impact on investment decisions (ibid., 461).

15. Some of Jackson's criticisms are noted in Bill Keller, "The Uneasiness between Blacks and Union Leaders," *New York Times* (May 13, 1984). Keller observes that an additional source of tension between black leadership and labor is the latter's opposition to enterprise zones and similar proposals for selectively reducing the minimum wage that have been endorsed by the National Conference of Black Mayors, the National Urban League, and other black groups.

16. In buttressing his claim to a more central role in Mondale's campaign, for example, Jackson complained; "The black vote has been more loyal to the Democratic Party than the Jewish vote or the labor vote, or any vote" ("Jackson Says Democrats Need Black Vote"). This invidious style was a recurrent feature of Jackson's initiative. He attacked the National Organization for Women for endorsing Mondale; the basis of his attack was an imponderable charge that NOW had stolen his campaign issue in pressing for nomination of a female vice-presidential candidate in the last weeks before the convention (Boyd, "Jackson Charges Mondale Ignored Him"). One day after his conciliatory convention speech Jackson struck a combative tone in telling black delegates that they had been shortchanged in political payoffs relative to other party constituencies. He maintained; "Women got the Vice Presidency. . . . The South got Bert Lance, New York got the keynoter and Manatt got the D.N.C. . . . And you got nothing" (Howell

Raines, "Assured Mondale Fights Rivals' Bids to Raid Delegates," *New York Times* [July 19, 1984]).

17. Iver Peterson, "Coors Seeks to Regain Cachet Using $625 Million Leverage," *New York Times* (November 16, 1984).

18. Ibid. The NAACP, Peterson notes, already had signed two dozen such "fair share agreements" with major corporations before the Coors pact.

Chapter 7

1. Harold Cruse observed this irony with regard to developing Black Power nationalism (*The Crisis of the Negro Intellectual* [New York, 1967], esp. 484). Cruse did not anticipate the circumstance, noted by sociologist Oliver Cox several years later, that the articulation of Black Power ideology toward ethnic pluralism—a development which Cruse advocated—was received favorably and reinforced by Jewish elites who had their own reasons to endorse an ethnic pluralist model for American group life. See Oliver C. Cox, "Jewish Self-interest in 'Black Pluralism,' " *Sociological Quarterly* 15 (Spring 1974): 183–98. In a separate critique Cox challenges the explanatory utility of pluralism as a mode of interpretation of American group dynamics in general ("The Question of Pluralism," *Race* 12 [Fourth Quarter 1971]: 385–400).

2. This observation corresponds to the descriptions of agenda formation processes generally operative in interest-group pluralism that have been proffered by Bachrach and Baratz, Stone, and others under such rubrics as "nondecision-making" or different "faces of power." In each case the focus is on the extent to which actual agenda setting depends on a prior—and politically consequential—delimitation of courses of action that can be considered "legitimate." See Peter Bachrach and Morton S. Baratz, *Power and Poverty: Theory and Practice* (New York, 1970), esp. 39–51; John Gaventa, *Power and Powerlessness* (Champaign-Urbana, 1980), 3–33; Steven Lukes, *Power: A Radical View* (London, 1974). Within this general approach Stone is perhaps clearest in distinguishing the ways in which systemic and relational constraints function ideologically to screen possibilities by determining the "logics of success and failure for individuals and institutions" (Clarence N. Stone, "Social Stratification, Nondecision-Making, and the Study of Community Power," *American Politics Quarterly* 10 [July 1982]: 275–302, and "Systemic Power in Community Decision Making: A Restatement of Stratification Theory," *American Political Science Review* 74 [December 1980]: 978–90).

3. This interpretation centers on the interaction of black and Jewish elites

within the status group structures legitimized in the Democratic coalition, where Jews and Afro-Americans function principally as such and not as proletarian activists, free-floating individuals committed to a just society or other competing identities.

4. See, for example, Ellen Hume, "Blacks and Jews Find Confrontation Rising over Jesse Jackson," *Wall Street Journal* (May 29, 1984). Irving Kristol characteristically was a principal ideologue of fissure, stating the line in "The Political Dilemma of American Jews," *Commentary* (July 1984).

5. Berman lists several of these in "Jackson and the Left," 407–08.

6. Arthur Hertzberg, "Behind Jews' Political Principles," *New York Times* (November 2, 1984). Indeed, if there were a reason to fear a mobilization of blacks on behalf of anti-Semitic purposes in the present period, it would lie in the propagation of the religio-political ideology that accompanies the mythology of the political church in the black community. Enlistment of black support for school prayer, anti-abortion politics, and so forth could increase the critical mass pushing for a dangerous Christian "purification" of the polity.

7. Hume, "Blacks and Jews."

8. Jews, in fact, were the only white religious group that Reagan did not carry in 1984, and he did not even run as well among Jewish voters (32 percent) as he had in 1980 (39 percent) (*"New York Times*/CBS News Poll: Portrait of the Electorate," *New York Times* [November 8, 1984]). For an analysis of Jewish voting patterns see Arthur Hertzberg, "Reagan and the Jews," *New York Review of Books* (January 31, 1985), 11–14.

9. Frances Fox Piven and Richard Cloward observe that while professional provider groups and recipients shared a common interest in expansion of the urban public service apparatus over the 1960s, the latter—especially the poor and dependent—constituted less a constituency of the former than a subordinate clientage. The demand for community control challenged this relation. See their essays in *The Politics of Turmoil* (New York, 1974). Lipsky examines the decisional and organizational logics that pattern the priorities of direct providers of human services (public safety, education, welfare, and so on) and their attitudes and behavior toward service recipients. He notes that those "street-level bureaucrats" often have considerable interpretive latitude at the point of execution of policy and program but are constrained primarily by imperatives deriving from bureaucratic and professional norms, rather than client interests (Michael Lipsky, *Toward a Theory of Street-Level Bureaucracy* [New York, 1980]).

10. The genesis and particulars of the dispute between the community school board and teachers' union are detailed—from a viewpoint generally

sympathetic to the parents—by the various contributions to Annette T. Rubinstein, ed., *Schools against Children* (New York, 1970).

11. John O'Neill, "The Rise and Fall of the UFT," in Rubenstein, *Schools against Children,* 181.

12. Rabbi Jay Kaufmann, "Thou Shalt Surely Rebuke Thy Neighbor," in James Baldwin et al., *Black Anti-Semitism and Jewish Racism* (New York, 1969), 44.

13. Ibid., 63.

14. Ibid., 52–53.

15. Ibid., 55. Compensatory affirmative action was only beginning to surface as a black demand.

16. Rabbi Alan W. Miller, "Black Anti-Semitism—Jewish Racism," in Baldwin et al., *Black Anti-Semitism,* 84.

17. Ibid., 93. In the same volume Karp and Shapiro recount the success of Shanker and other opponents of decentralization in mobilizing Jewish support—which had been mixed—on their behalf by propagating hysteria over the red herring of black anti-Semitism (Walter Karp and H. R. Shapiro, "Exploding the Myth of Black Anti-Semitism," in Baldwin et al., 129–41). Noting the flimsiness of the Anti-Defamation League's dossier alleging evidence of rampant anti-Semitism, Karp and Shapiro observe that "any black failure to compliment Jewish teachers [was presented as] bigotry" (137).

18. Albert Vorspan "Blacks and Jews," in Baldwin et al., *Black Anti-Semitism,* 220–21.

19. Ibid., 204.

20. Ibid., 200–04.

21. Ibid., 208.

22. Ibid., 216. He asks whether it is "tolerable that the flag of anti-Semitism shall be run up whenever it is Jews who are asked to give up some power?" (217).

23. William Raspberry, "The Cost of Jackson's Slur," *Washington Post* (March 2, 1984).

24. Cited in Hume, "Blacks and Jews."

25. Albert Vorspan, "Blacks, Jews and Tensions in New Rochelle: Longtime Allies 'Joined at the Hip,' " *New York Times* (September 23, 1984).

26. Joseph Berger, "Jewish Leaders Criticize Jackson: The Democrats Are Also Warned," *New York Times* (July 11, 1984).

27. William G. Blair, "Jewish Leaders Hail Jackson Unity Plea but Voice Caution," *New York Times* (July 19, 1984). Perlmutter noted that Jackson attacked South Africa but not the others. The reverse standard easily could

be applied to Jewish elites who refuse to criticize Israel's support of South Africa.

28. Vorspan, "Blacks and Jews," 217.

29. Miller, "Black Anti-Semitism," 96.

30. Harold Cruse, "My Jewish Problem and Theirs," in Baldwin et al., *Black Anti-Semitism,* 184.

31. The contending positions—in the aftermath of Reagan's reelection—are exemplified in the exchange by Peter Rosenblatt and Michael Calabrese, "The Election's Lessons for the Democrats," *New York Times* (November 19, 1984).

Chapter 8

1. Howell Raines, "Jackson Poses Some Difficult Questions for Other Democrats," *New York Times* (November 6, 1983). Raines, author of a journalistic history of the era, commented that those rallies "recalled the civil rights movement where Mr. Jackson started as an aide to Dr. King in the Southern Christian Leadership Conference."

2. For discussions of Jackson's media style see Barbara Reynolds, *Jesse Jackson,* passim, and Les Payne, "Black Reporters, White Press—And the Jackson Campaign," *Columbia Journalism Review* (July/August 1984): 32–37. Reynolds cites at least two instances between 1972 and 1975 in which Jackson denounced black reporters who had written articles critical of some of his activities as "Black Judases" (*Jesse Jackson,* 406). The Milton Coleman incident was, therefore, not without precedent.

3. Payne, "Black Reporters, White Press," 36.

4. Kalb's query is quoted in ibid.

5. This muteness is exemplified in the absence of black leadership from the lively debate over the Democratic party's future that followed Reagan's reelection. Although much of this debate centered on proposals that the party retreat from its identification with labor, racial minorities, and a commitment to social welfare, black spokesmen—including Jackson—were conspicuous as nonparticipants, opting instead to maintain visibility in a series of well-orchestrated, celebrity protests against South Africa.

For examples of the postelection discussion see Morton W. Kondracke, "Democrats' Next Chairman Must Unite Four 'Parties,' " *Wall Street Journal* (November 15, 1984); Ronald Smothers, "Democrats Look to Their Demographics," *New York Times* (December 2, 1984); Ellen Hume, "Democrats Seek Comeback Chief," *Wall Street Journal* (November 19, 1984); Peter R. Rosenblatt, "Centrism Is Crucial," and Michael A. Calabrese, "In Illinois, Economics," *New York Times* (November 19, 1984); Leonard M. Apcar, "Defeated Labor Tries to Regroup," *Wall Street Journal* (November 23, 1984); William Serrin, "Kirkland Stresses Solidarity on Candidate Endorsement," *New York Times* (December 2, 1984); Tom Wicker, "A Party of Access?" *New York Times* (November 25, 1984); Kevin Phillips, "Old Political Labels No Longer Fit," *Wall Street Journal* (November 27, 1984); Richard C. Wade, "Why Voters Have Grown Independent," *New York Times* (December 12, 1984); and Gordon Rayfield and Julian Bain, "Don't Take Yuppies for Granted," *New York Times* (November 16, 1984). Jackson first indicated after the election that rather than joining the fray over Democratic reorganization, he intended to concentrate on building his fictive Rainbow; then—climbing aboard the recently formed bandwagon—he announced his plan to travel to South Africa to "visit with church leaders, labor leaders, [and] government officials." See E. R. Shipp, "Jackson to Put Energies into Political Coalition," *New York Times* (November 20, 1984), and "Jesse Jackson Says He Is Pressing South Africa for Talks on Policies," *New York Times* (December 3, 1984).

6. Among recent critiques of the premise of media neutrality at least two are especially persuasive. See Todd Gitlin, *The Whole World Is Watching: Mass Media in the Making and Unmaking of the New Left* (Berkeley, 1980), and Ben Bagdikian, *Media Monopoly* (Boston, 1983). Gitlin painstakingly describes the intersection of the media's logic of newsworthiness and the New Left's impetus to expansion and argues that the interpenetration of those two logics shaped the growth and decline of activism in the late 1960s. Bagdikian brings into prominence the often obscured fact that the media are themselves creatures of corporate capital—and act accordingly.

7. "Jesse Jackson's Victory," *New York Times* (May 28, 1984).

8. Frederick Allen, "Jackson Factor Leaves Black Leaders Uncertain, Fearful," *Atlanta Constitution* (August 12, 1984).

9. Ibid.

10. Perkins, "Are Black Leaders Listening to Black America?" *Wall Street Journal* (October 16, 1984).

11. "Jesse Jackson Has Special Obligation to His Followers," *Atlanta Journal* (April 23, 1984).

12. Barry Commoner, "Jackson's Historic Campaign," *New York Times*, (July 10, 1984).

13. Philip Green, "The Reality beneath the Rainbow," *The Nation* (March 17, 1984).

14. Berman, "Jackson and the Left." Berman had raised questions concerning Jackson's history of opportunism and flirtation with Republi-

cans, past association with right-wing social policy positions, and anti-Semitism.

15. Philip Green, "Reply," *The Nation* (April 7, 1984), 411. Green's reply was among the earliest and most cogent responses to the anti-Semitism issue.

16. Ibid., 410.

17. Kopkind, "Black Power in the Age of Jackson," 535.

18. Ibid., 538–39.

19. Ibid., 541.

20. Ibid., 539.

21. Wilkins, "The Natural." Here I should recall that within the black community the Jackson motion spawned a similar byproduct to the extent that the campaign served as a source of encouragement and a springboard for peripheral political aspirants.

22. A response to this interpretation might be that the campaign did solicit and prepare position papers on a variety of domestic and international issues. However, there is little indication that those documents were integrated to inform a coherent agenda for governing; nor were they projected publicly—certainly not in the black community—as constitutive of an electoral platform. Instead, it seems very much that for Jackson—reminiscent of Andrew Young's posture in his bid for election to the House of Representatives as well as a wider practice among black officeseekers—formal policy positions were incidental and were useful mainly generically, to be cited in reply to criticisms that the campaign lacked purposive political vision.

23. The problem here is with neither the usefulness of application of ethnic interest-group models to black politics nor with the empirical content, so far as it goes, of the results of their application. The strength of this approach is that it adumbrates the mechanisms of blacks' integration into the American system of group politics and to that extent demystifies the relation of black political activity to the national political culture. Rather, the problem is that this mode of interpretation focuses not so much on identifying the logics typical of Afro-American politics as on calculating the extent to which certain of its properties conform to a prior constructs developed in other contexts. In the last analysis this problem is intrinsic to the idea of a conceptual model, which is a device that—however useful— ultimately tends to order the world of lived experience imperialistically, in line with an emphasis on discovering regularities. The concern with regularities entails a focus that by definition is extrinsic to particular situations and tends to subordinate the latter's specificity to the requirements of an idee fixe, often in a way that is suspiciously analogical. More specifically,

with regard to interpretation of Afro-American politics, the incompleteness of this approach is concealed by general cultural presumptions that deny the value of examination of autonomous political dynamics among blacks.

24. Cruse, *Crisis of the Negro Intellectual,* esp. 147–301, and *Rebellion or Revolution?* (New York, 1968), 126–55.

25. See, for example, Richard Wright, *American Hunger* (New York, 1977) and *The Outsider* (New York, 1953), and Ralph Ellison, *Invisible Man* (New York, 1952) and several of his essays in *Shadow and Act* (New York, 1964).

26. Ellison, "The World and the Jug," in *Shadow and Act,* 123.

27. Kopkind, "Black Power in the Age of Jackson," 539.

28. This problem has been intensified by the atrophy of an indigenous realm for black political debate in the 1970s and 1980s, as the only viable terrain for critical commentary on Afro-American politics has become situated increasingly in the institutions of the Left.

Index

Reed resents the fact that
J.J. was chosen by blocks
instead of others? p. 111

1) moral dilemma
2) modernization
3) Colonialism
4) power relations